Anthology
2017

COVINGTON WRITERS GROUP

COVINGTON WRITERS GROUP
ANTHOLOGY 2017

Jenny Breeden, Managing Editor
Gary Reed and Mikey Chlanda, Proofreading Editors

ISBN: 1-945368-05-5
ISBN-13: 978-1-945368-05-9

PUBLISHED BY COVINGTON WRITERS GROUP, INC.
IN CONJUNCTION WITH
SEAGULL PRODUCTIONS LLC
COVINGTON, KY 41014

AUTHOR RIGHTS

TABLE OF CONTENTS

ACKNOWLEDGMENTS

Covington Writers Group thanks our supporters:

Roebling Point Books and Coffee, on 3rd and Greenup in Covington, for providing a friendly environment whenever we needed an additional or alternative meeting place. We further thank them for offering our books for sale, and on display in their reading rooms.

The staff at Zola Pub and Grill in MainStrasse Village, Covington, for providing us with their spacious second floor dining area on the second and fourth Saturday evenings each month, so we can socialize and critique stories in a friendly and lively environment.

The Center for Great Neighborhoods (CGN) for welcoming us into their community building. Eager to partner with small creative businesses, the CGN is a catalyst for positive growth in Covington, and an exciting opportunity for our group. We meet in their board room on the first and third Saturday mornings of each month.

INTRODUCTION

The Covington Writers Group marked its fourth year as an active group in 2017. Our members spent most of the year working on our own writing projects, some for this anthology and others for publication as stand-alone works. A half dozen of our members had their work published or received notifications their work had been accepted for future publication. It was one of our most productive years.

In October, we partnered with the Boone County Public Library, Main Branch to celebrate the Second Annual Indie Author Day. The day's events included a presentation by local author, Orville Mann, a panel discussion featuring our group's most prolific published author, Mikey Chlanda, and a book fair with more than thirty-five local authors making their books available to the public.

Our poems and stories in this edition were peer reviewed during our monthly meetings to improve our writing skills. They are a diverse collection from many genres, some enriched with our members' personal memories. We hope you enjoy our anthology.

The members of Covington Writers Group express their heartfelt thanks to our family and friends, for allowing us to spend some of our time away from them while we write, share our work at group meetings, and grow as writers. Their love and sacrifices mean the world to us as we strive for success.

POETRY

THE PROMISE

By *Kimberly Armstrong*

There is something between us. You may or may not know it yet.
Born of proximity. Attraction. Loneliness.
A whispering wanting, that makes itself known
Only in the dead of night.
This is something dangerous
That instantly pokes my ears up for signs of what could hurt.

You know I see you, don't you?
Looking at me...once or twice
I have no idea what you see behind those eyes.

There are always warm hellos and goodbyes
Hugs one would think would soothe the savage breast
Still, I cannot get enough.

You know I see you, right?
Acting like nothing's different, nothing's changed.
Tiny things are your tell.

Each person is different.
Some will write you songs; put forth dramatic displays.
Yours are quiet. Barely noticeable.

All of them converge to form one silent message
Only we two see transmitted
Passing through the invisible ether hung between us.

The way you got up once and came to sit next to me
Perfectly silently
The pull--that pull--I thought only I could feel.

You are near; I want you nearer still
I want. I want. The void says, More.
Black hole eating light.

I touch your knee
Your hand slides down your thigh and finds mine
My whole body goes warm inside
Because someone cute – a boy!
Held my hand under the table.

You are normal. I am a seeker.
Does your void speak to you equally?

One day it will come to pass.
I feel it like old bones sense a change in barometric pressure.
What was innocent will turn.
What brought joy will lead to disappointment and resentment.
I recognize this day as the day I will likely lose you.
Not for your desire to leave.

Rather, for my need to set you free.

Know that I will protect you.
From me.
Even from you.

This is a promise I will keep.

TO THE STATE-SPONSORED TERRORIST

By *Kimberly Armstrong*

This poem is dedicated to all those who have fallen victim to state-sponsored terrorism. To all those who live in states that sponsor militarism, racism, authoritarianism, and unaccountable corporate rule. And, lastly, to all those who long for peace.

Inspired by Alden Solovy's "To the Terrorist" as seen on ritualwell.com.

We who have been denied the presence of our native sisters and
brothers
We who sense the emptiness around us in the land and in our souls
But cannot quite pinpoint the cause

We miss the richness they would have brought to our lives and our
communities
We who live in colonial states still in the making
We who live in colonial states that have made it

You who stain the rivers with petroleum and poor people's blood
You who rain down bombs on weddings and funerals
You who see our mothers, babies, uncles and neighbors as acceptable
collateral damage

We, the children who play in fields littered with depleted uranium
We who seek shelter in schools and hospitals to no avail

We know the truth that bombs don't rain down hugs and love

You who in your suits and ties and other fine dress wear
Decide who will live and who will die
As though each human being were not an irreplaceable universe of
our own

You who attempt to divide our solidarity for your own profit
You who steal, rape, and pillage in the name of religion and nation
Who harden hearts to reason, science, and love

Know this: we hear the drums of justice beating, calling
An insistence that will not be silenced by propaganda
We answer the call for all peoples and nations to stand together

To defend the land, the water, the plants and animals
With our votes, our protests and our bodies, if we are so able
With our prayers, our voices and our perseverance--because we must

Though we are not free to desist from this work
We choose to decide not with fear but with hope
Invoking that which goes beyond ourselves and is without end

The long arc of history bends toward justice not on its own
But because the human spirit compels it
And the human conscience demands we make it so.

LETTER TO ROBERT

By *Patti Kay Emerson*

My Dear Robert,

It has been seven years
Since you left this world,
But it seems like seven minutes.
I love you as I always did.

I miss you so much
and wish I could see you,
But for now, your picture must suffice
Until it is my time to join you
In that lovely place
Where you are now.

I think of you often,
As I watch the Cincinnati Reds play
And at special times of the year,
Such as Christmas and your birthday,
Which are the same day,
And the anniversary of our engagement,
Just nine days before your final journey took place.

I remember how you and my dad
Used to talk to each other about the Reds games.
I can imagine the two of you together
Watching the games from Heaven
And that makes me happy

With all my love,

Patti

In memory of Robert J. Anstead 12/25/1951 – 8/19/2010

MY SISTER

By *Patti Kay Emerson*

My sister, Mary, was a loving woman.
She loved her family: daughter, grandchildren, great-grandchildren,
And siblings with all her heart
She worked for many years
As a registered nurse
Taking care of strangers, who became family to her.

She especially liked to work with the children
She was old enough to be my mother
And sometimes when she talked to me
It seemed she thought she was.

She was active in her church
Until she was unable to go.
She liked to watch religious shows
Such as the Bill Gaither Classic Music Reunions, Charles Stanley, and
Billy Graham
And the Cincinnati Reds
All who knew her will surely miss her.

In memory of Mary Ruth Alborg, 9/14/1938 – 9/9/2017

FRIENDS

By *Patti Kay Emerson*

You may think that no one cares
But you'll always have friends somewhere.
In your loneliest hours, your friends are there.
You may not see them
But when you need them most, they're always there.
Friends are very caring people.
In your happiest hour, they're always there.
Even when they aren't visible
Friends are always there.
When you need someone to talk to
Showing they care, they're always there.
Even when they know you are wrong
Friends still support you there.
Even if they too are suffering
Reaching out, they'll still be there.
In your saddest times
Your friends are always there.
You do not have to be at home to find friends like these.
Wherever you are, friends are there.
You can find them at work or school,
At church, or even in the hospital.
Wherever you are in life, whether sick or well,
True friends are always there.

ODE TO MY MIND AND HEART

By *Elle Mott*

My mind
Gutsy, persistent, assured, passionate, brave,

Once expected to live up to family standards
Now I'm gutsy to be me,

Once inundated with abnormal social norms of prejudice
Now I'm persistent to accept and love differences,

Once indoctrinated by religious nuances
Now I'm assured with non-mythical reason,

Once okay to hate or so I was told
Now I'm passionate to love,

Once told it is what it is
Now I'm brave to make change,

Gutsy, persistent, assured, passionate, brave
My mind, and my heart.

SONGS FROM LISNAFAER

By *L. N. Passmore*

Excerpted from *Wayward Wulves Beware*, Book One of the Eye of the Wulf Series, available at amazon.com. Visit L. N. Passmore's website at www.lnpassmore.com for more tales of Lisnafaer or see Covington Writers *Anthology 2016*, available at amazon.com.

A CALL TO ADVENTURE

[Lady Light in her guise as White Wulf sings to lure Sonsie, a young wulf who yearns to be a great wulf singer, to the Cavern Perilous.]

> "Come wee wulf, come and play,
> Way down the little derry-do, up the rocky hillock.
> Ah, what treasures, yours to find, deep within the hiding hole?
> Solas, Dorcha—or much worse?
> Ancient tunes oft hide a curse.
> Come bold wulf, come and run,
> Behind the bristly tricksy-tree, through the tumbly torrents.
> Ah, what faer songs, yours to hear, just beyond the crinkle-crack?
> Solas, Dorcha—or much worse?
> Ancient tunes oft hide a curse.
> Come brave wulf, come and leap,
> Over the grackly springle-sprat, past the weepy willow run.
> Ah, what secrets, yours to learn, just across the flaming stream?
> Solas, Dorcha—or much worse?
> Ancient tunes oft hide a curse."

BLESSED LISNAFAER

[Sonsie sings a song he could have heard only from some
supernatural source.]

"Each night, haroo, hoorae
    Gealach, sweet Silver-Light, pure and bright,
    Calls starlight from the black depths of night,
    Draws light from the vasty dark sae cold.
    Ferlie the lights of the Ladies sae auld.

Each dawn, haroo, hoorae
    Silv'ry Sister-Light, lovely the sight,
    Sings to Grian, Fire-Light, hot and bright,
    Sends light Mother-Light spins into gold.
    Ferlie the lights of the Ladies sae auld.

Each day, haroo, hoorae
    Great Grian, our Gold-Mother, splendid might,
    Makes sweet Change, breathes golden life from light,
    Sings hallowed story, each day retold.
    Ferlie the lights of the Ladies sae auld.

All day, haroo, hoorae
    Great Grian, our Gold-Mother, meet and right,
    Bathes Lisnafaer with her love-light,
    Frees Lisnafaer from death's leasehold.
    Ferlie the lights of the Ladies sae auld.

Night and day, haroo, hoorae
    Light grows. Love grows. Life grows.
    So Love is: giving and taking, dying and living.
    Queen Grian, Blessed Mother-Light, calls the children:
    Beasts in caves and dens and lairs,
    Lord Green lost in burrow grim,
    Deep down under wulfways.
    Doleful Lady Light, seeks her Lord,
    With his arm strong and staff firm.
    Mother-Light sends love, sweet and warm,
    Dries her tears, lights her way.
    Love-Light shines.
    Light laughs into Green.
    So Love is: calling and seeking, returning and blessing
    Lisnafaer."

[*Gealach*—moon; *sae*—so; ferlie—wondrous, marvelous; *Grian*—sun]

BYE, BYE, BUTTERFLY

By *Gary Reed*

With help from Josie Benton, age 10

Josie's Papaw had a very nice farm.
There, Josie saw a Monarch butterfly.
Papaw said, "It's pretty and does no harm,
"But Josie, if you touch it, it will die."

"Where does the Monarch butterfly come from?"
She asked. Papaw said he didn't know.
"They like pollen and they take a tiny crumb
From plant to plant, and they help my crops grow."

So, Josie hurried to the library.
She read, and she read, and she read and read.
She learned all about the butterfly.
She kept so many facts in her head!

"Oh, look, it's a pretty Monarch butterfly!"
"It flew here all the way from Mexico."
She told her Mamaw, when one zipped by.
"To help Papaw's corn and green beans grow."

Then, one June, she didn't see the Monarch.
She did not see even one in the sky,
Or in Papaw's farm, or in Big Bone park.
Where was the pretty Monarch butterfly?

So, Josie hurried to the library.
She read, and she read, and she read and read
To learn more about the butterfly.
She kept so many facts in her head!

She found out why the Monarch did not show.
President Trump built a very long wall
Along the border with Mexico.
It kept the Monarch out, it was so tall!

9 ACROSS, HUMMINGBIRDS

By *Gary Reed*

The little hummingbird fluttered
Just over the *New York Times* crossword
Puzzle and silently muttered.
It tried hard to think of the right word

For "Nearly Extinct Pollinators":
One that ended in the letter "s".
A word with exactly twelve letters.
Alas, the little bird couldn't guess.

SALVADOR DALÍ & HIS OCELOT

By *Gary Reed*

Salvador Dalí was a very big deal
In modern art. His paintings sold for a lot,
And his long, pointed mustache was just unreal.
But you know, they say he kept an ocelot
As a pet. Can you imagine? How surreal!

Dalí may have been loved by the jet set,
But I think he was more than a little bent.
I mean, he kept an ocelot as a pet
And took the darned thing wherever he went!

PHOOEY TO CHOP SUEY

By *Gary Reed*

We took our favorite grandson
To the Tai Shan Magic Dragon
Chinese Buffet one Saturday,
To celebrate his fifth birthday.
But Danny was in a terrible mood
And refused to eat the food.

We said, "How about Chop Suey?"
Mean, rotten Danny said, "Phooey!"
We asked the little birthday troll,
"How about fried rice in a bowl?"

Danny pouted and said, "No dice!
I don't want a bunch of fried rice!"

"Would you like a nice spring egg roll?
We just got the same rigmarole.
"How about fried rice-paddy eel?"
Danny let out a horrible squeal.

We tried to get the little dork
To eat some tasty Moo Shu pork,
But he just shouted, "No, no, no!"
He refused the Chow Mein also.

The waitress brought out the cook,
Who grabbed our Danny and took
Him to the kitchen. "Don't squawk,
Or I'll put you in a big wok
With garlic and some fresh Bok
Choy, and put you on the menu!
Tell me, what's the matter with you."

Danny said, "It's my fifth birthday.
I just want to have fun today."

"You want some fun, Little Dragon?
I make you my special How Fun!"

FREE CRUISE!

By *Gary Reed*

Imagine Noah's shock when dinosaurs
Showed up expecting a free cruise!
Giant lizards asking about tours,
Shore excursions, and windows with views!

Disgruntled, jet-lagged dinosaurs,
Expecting a giant new cruise ship,
Thought Noah's tents and Ark were eyesores.
"Just wait," they said, "till we rate this trip!"

First, Trent and Trixie Triceratops
Showed up out of the clear blue sky
Wearing only sun screen and flip flops.
Not even good old Noah knew why.

And then there was Bob Brontosaurus,
Who'd just learned he'd won a free cruise.
"A telemarketer phoned us,"
His wife said, "with the exciting news."

"He told us we could get a free meal
"And learn about a lovely time-share.
"The price is practically a steal.
"It's in the Yucatan or somewhere."

"But Bob doesn't want to be hurried
"Into something he'll regret later.
"This talk of a flood has him worried.
"What if property values crater?"

The mighty Tyrannosaurus Rex
And his lovely wife, T. Regina,
Demanded rooms on the upper decks
And tutors for the Macarena.

Hailing from the Early Cretaceous,
Karl Krytops, an Episcopalian,
Escorted his wife, the bodacious
Kathy, a vegetarian.

Kathy Krytops demanded to know:
"Is it true that Elvis Presley
"Will perform the after-dinner show?
"And this is Coke. Can we get Pepsi?"

The always so-thoughtful-and-gracious
Charlie and Cynthia Ceratops,
Arrived from the Late Cretaceous,
"Does the Ark," they asked, "have bellhops?"

So it went, one pair for each species,
Flintstone dinosaurs by the thousands,
Mountains of smelly dino feces –
Noah grumbled, "It just never ends!"

THE PANDA COMMA COMMOTION

By *Gary Reed*

"That's him," Steve, the diner's proprietor, said.
"The Panda with the Santa hat on his head.
"Every day, it's the same: He eats shoots and leaves.
"Next, I'm afraid, he'll eat my holiday wreaths."

The police arrested the chubby Panda
And dutifully read him his Miranda
Rights. "This Giant Panda eats, shoots, and leaves,"
They wrote, "He was disturbing the peace at Steve's."

"Eating shoots and leaves is not a felony,"
The Panda said. "I don't need an attorney.
"What I need now is for you to call Lynn Truss.
I'm sure she can easily explain the fuss."

"And, kind Sir, please be sure to tell the warden,"
The Panda continued, "that I'm a vegan.
I need a lot of bamboo in my diet."
"Oh, shut up!" the cop replied. "Just be quiet."

A rowdy bystander began to complain,
"That Panda's going to be a royal pain,
"I say, just shoot the stupid tree hugger!"
"Don't you dare!" said a Sierra Club member.

Now, here's the thing: The Panda was black *and* white,
So, the police officers really were not quite
Sure: The Giant Panda's white, cut it some slack?
Or, the big Panda's black, shoot it in the back?

The Panda cried out: "Black-and-white lives matter!"
Lynn Truss arrived and said, "Commas matter!"
Local rappers put it to hip hop music:
"We need justice for the monochromatic!"

At the nearby Zoo, an African zebra
And a pair of skunks took up the mantra:
Don't shoot the Panda! Black-and-white lives matter!"
The grammarian replied. "Commas Matter!"

A rare white tiger growled; a snowy owl
Hooted; and a lemur said it in a howl:
"Don't shoot the Panda! Black-and-white lives matter!"
But Truss was adamant: "Commas matter!"

At the scene, a police sergeant scowled.
At the firehouse, a proud Dalmatian growled:
"Don't shoot the Panda! Black-and-white lives matter!"
Lynn Truss still insisted: "Commas matter!"

The harried police called the dispatcher.
A passing street preacher shouted, "It's the Rapture!"
The crowd chanted, "Black-and-white lives matter!"
The dispatcher concluded this was the matter:

"At Steve's Exotic Bamboo Emporium
"There's Panda-Comma Pandemonium."

AN OCELOT OUGHT NOT DRIVE A LOT

By *Gary Reed*

It could hardly have been much clearer,
Back when that very first ocelot
Attempted to drive an old junker
Off a South Texas used-car lot:
An ocelot's not much of driver;
It would end badly, likely as not.

If it stands erect on the front seat
So it can see over the dashboard,
It cannot reach the brakes with its feet.
And if it crawls up on the floorboard,
It can't steer or even see the street.
The used car guy didn't say a word!

That first ocelot chose an old Ford,
(It was about all it could afford),
And then, down the highway it roared,
No driver's license, uninsured,
Over the speed limit, right toward
An old gasoline tanker... Oh, Lord!

A BLUE CATERPILLAR

By *Gary Reed*

A large, blue caterpillar,
Its appearance singular,
Sat on its plump, royal tosh
In a mulberry bush
And smoked rutabaga
Leaf in a golden hookah.

"Someday, you will fly,"
Alice said.
"I'll be high,"
It responded,
And absconded
With her prime stash
Of 'baga hash.

A MOTHER'S PRAYER

By *Alvena Stanfield*

Give my children joy
Show my husband their splendor
Soften his rage
Enlighten me which decision
To choose, best for them
I want nothing for myself.

Change their teachers' fierce approach
Toward studied lessons not learned
Halt their classmates' attacks
Cure my daughter's disease
Overcome her coordination and dyslexia challenges
I want nothing for myself.

Guide them toward satisfying careers
Send them honest, loving spouses
Strike down her child-molesting husband
Open her eyes to see his evil
Keep him in prison
I want nothing for myself.

Increase her courage as he threatens
Cure my other daughter's cancer
Save her from excruciating pain
Stop her husband's apathy
Don't let her die alone
I want nothing for myself.

Allow her to raise her daughter
Teach her to walk again
Ease her pain
Don't let my other one die alone
Cure my husband's cancer
I want nothing for myself.

I, wearing a smile for a shield,
Held onto blind faith, and hope.
Does God know what mattered
Know why they mattered.
Asking nothing for myself.
God gave exactly that. Nothing.

FICTION

SCUTTLEBUTT LANE

By *Jenny Breeden*

Blood-curdling screams coming from the open windows of the Malloy house next door pierced the silence of what had been a peaceful Tuesday night. They woke me up from a sound sleep. Shouting, glass breaking, and door slamming were sure to follow as they usually did when Dean and Jessie got into one of their "arguments." That's what Jessie called them in her futile attempt to save face, but the rest of the neighborhood knew they were knock-down, drag out fights. From the sound of it, this one was going to be another doozy.

I hoped it wouldn't be as bad as the one last month when the police had to come break it up. They were ready to arrest Dean for assault when Jessie convinced them that he never hit her.

"If you had any sense," Kathy, another neighbor, had told her several times before, "you'd leave his useless butt and take him to the cleaners in the divorce settlement."

But no, Jesse stayed with him. She just kept making excuses for him and putting herself back into harm's way. New to the neighborhood, I didn't really know all the gory details, so I wasn't making any judgments. In truth, I didn't know who was to blame for their troubled marriage. In my experience, it usually took two to tango. They were probably both to blame for the mess they'd gotten themselves into.

I sat on the edge of my bed for a minute. As I expected, the initial screams weren't the end of it. I got up and put on my sweat pants and a robe, so I'd be presentable when I stepped outside on my porch.

Grabbing my cellphone off the charger, I headed down the steps. The time displayed on the tiny screen ... 11:23 PM. *At least I got about thirty minutes of sleep before all this started.*

Gloria Wilson, the neighbor on the other side of the Malloy house, had called the police the last several times, so if things got ugly, it was probably my turn to call 911. I stepped out on my front porch at the same time as Bill Jenkins did across the street.

"Wonderful night for a moon dance," I called across to him, pointing at the July full moon glowing brightly in the bluish-black sky above the cul-de-sac.

Bill lit a cigarette, "I couldn't sleep anyway ... too damn quiet in this neighborhood."

We both laughed.

Suddenly the Malloy's front door flew open and Dean came bounding out onto the porch and down the steps. "You can't throw me out, you bitch! I'm leaving before you hurt yourself again, and I end up in jail because of your lies. Pack your things and get out of MY house!"

"I'm not leaving, you bastard," Jessie screeched, standing in the open doorway. "I gave you the last ten years, I deserve something in return ... so I'm keeping the house and everything in it."

"You'll play hell getting it. It's mine!" He headed for his car in the driveway, turned and yelled, "I'll burn it down before I'd let you have it."

Jessie came flying out the door with something in her hand and flung it hard in Dean's direction. It must have been glass or ceramic because it shattered when it hit the ground a few feet from the front end of the car.

"You bitch! I've had it with you," he screamed. "You've got two hours, then I'm coming back with the cops to put your nasty ass out."

I hadn't heard them carrying on like this before. Certainly, nothing about burning down the house. Something must have happened to set them off.

Everything seemed normal when I went to bed around ten to watch the early news and weather. But then again, I hadn't been in this neighborhood long enough to know what was normal.

I had decided to move after my husband died eight months ago. That big, older house of ours was too much to handle on my own ... too many things needed attention, like the roof, siding, and furnace. Although there were many good times spent in the house raising our twin sons, James and John and our daughter, Judy, it held too many sad memories ... the day uniformed Marines appeared at the door to advise we'd lost James in Iraq ... coming home from the hospital after losing Judy and our third grandchild to complications of childbirth ... watching my true love Harry lose his battle to cancer. I desperately needed a change of scenery.

My real estate agent found me a great two-story, three-bedroom house in a newer neighborhood on the edge of downtown with an in-ground pool in the back yard. Plenty of room for me to have a home office and a guest room, for when John and his wife, Angie, came to visit or when my son-in-law Marc let my two grandkids stay for the weekend.

"All the conveniences of being in town without the traffic and noise," the agent said as her main selling point.

She was right too. The house was on a short street with a cul-de-sac, which meant little to no traffic. Only people who had a reason to be there ever drove down the street.

I used the better part of the check I'd received from Harry's life insurance to purchase a "little peace and quiet." That was four months ago and so far, it was anything but quiet.

I'm an outgoing person. I immediately made friends with the middle-forties couple, Kathy and Bill Jenkins, and their fifteen-year-old twin boys, Eric and Aaron. Their house was directly across the street from mine. Kathy and I hit it off right away because we had so much in common, including having twin boys.

Kathy introduced me to Jessie, and I eventually met her husband Dean. Even though Kathy and I got along great, Jessie and I never really hit it off. Kathy and Jessie had lived in the neighborhood together for about a decade and had become close friends. At one point, Kathy laughingly suggested that maybe Jessie didn't warm up to me because she thought I was stealing her "best friend" away from her, since I was always sitting on Kathy's front porch or she was relaxing in or around my pool. The way Jessie looked at me sometimes, I was beginning to believe she really was jealous.

Lately though, Jessie seemed to be friendlier and would come over to talk with me even if Kathy wasn't there. I only talked to Dean if he was in the yard or driveway. Even that earned me dirty looks from Jessie if she was home and paying attention. I was a recent widow who was still in love with her husband, and Dean was married. Jessie didn't have anything to worry about on my account. But jealousy can make a person think crazy things.

The Robinson family lived on the other side of Gloria's house. Alice and Jim were in their late 30's with five children, two boys and three girls. From my pool deck, I could see them playing in the yard on their swing set or running around the house. They seemed like a happy family, but they were noisy ... yelling to one another while playing tag or hide-n-seek, laughing and singing. The kind of noise you like to hear in a neighborhood. Not like what we'd just heard coming from the Malloy's next door.

During the commotion, Kathy joined Bill on the porch. When Dean's car sped up the street and out of sight, everything got quiet again. "Hey Lisa, I just opened a bottle before all the excitement started," she said, raising her glass in my direction. "Want to come over and help me kill it?"

"Might as well." I headed down the steps and strolled across the street. "Looks like they ruined my chances of going back to sleep anytime soon." When I got to their porch, Kathy was alone, holding two full glasses. "Not sure what to make of all that," I said in a quieter voice. I didn't want Jessie or the other neighbors to hear me.

Kathy shook her head and handed me a glass. "I know. Jessie hasn't said anything recently about them having any trouble. As a matter of fact, she was telling me just last week about her plans to do something special to celebrate their tenth anniversary. It's coming up at the beginning of August."

"I'm curious to see what happens when Dean comes back ... you know, if he'll bring the police and if he'll really try to put her out in the middle of the night."

"That's why I want to stay up for a while. If Jessie does pack a few things to leave, she won't have any place to go. Besides Dean took the car. If she did want to go someplace, she'd have to call someone to come get her. I'm her best friend, so I'm thinking she may want to come over here for the night." Kathy took a sip of wine and shook her head. "I can't imagine what she's going through."

Sitting on the porch talking, we didn't notice the sky clouding up. When it started to rain around midnight, we were both somewhat surprised but not concerned; her porch had a nice roof, and the rain was coming straight down with no wind. After a few minutes, it changed from a medium rain to a torrential downpour.

"This rain sure did pop up all of a sudden. I don't recall hearing anything in the forecast about rain for tonight, did you?"

Kathy took another sip of wine before responding. "No, but you know our weather, unpredictable, especially in the middle of summer."

As quickly as it started raining, it stopped. About fifteen minutes altogether, just enough time to soak everything. *Hopefully, it dries up as quickly, I thought, so I don't have to get my feet and pant legs all wet walking home.*

At 12:45 AM, I was trying to decide if I should go home or not when Kathy offered the use of her facilities. I didn't want to wake up Bill or her boys, but I figured it would be faster to duck into her house than to head across the street to mine. I just got back to the porch when Dean's car drove up and pulled into the driveway.

He sat in his car for a few minutes until he saw the police car approaching with its blue lights flashing. He got out and glared over at the two of us. He stood there in silence until the police car parked in the cul-de-sac in front of his house. The two officers exited their car and walked up to meet him.

Pointing his finger at us, he yelled, "I knew you nosy bitches couldn't resist waiting up to see the fireworks. Well, I warned her. She'd better be gone ... I brought reinforcements."

One of the police officers said, "Now sir, we don't want any trouble tonight. If your wife is still here, we will ask her to leave voluntarily. If she refuses, we can take her into custody if you file a complaint that she assaulted you."

"Ok, let's go," Dean said. "I want to get this over with, so I can get some sleep. I have to work in the morning."

Rapping hard on the door, the officer announced loudly, "Police, Mrs. Malloy, we need to talk to you."

"Jessie, you get your ass out here right now!" Dean screamed.

"Mr. Malloy, please stand back," one of the officer said. "We said we don't want any trouble."

"Well she's asking for trouble 'cuz she's not coming out. You'll have to go in and get her."

"We're not even sure she's still here," the first officer said.

"Ask them," he said, pointing over at us again. "I'll bet them nosy bitches over there have been watching my house since I left. They'll tell you she's still in there."

The second officer walked over to Kathy's porch. When he was close enough, he asked, "Did either of you see Mrs. Malloy leave the house after Mr. Malloy left?"

Kathy piped up first. "I've been out here since he drove off and I haven't seen her come out since she went back into the house a couple of hours ago."

"And you ma'am, what did you see?"

"I didn't see her come out either." I thought about telling him I wasn't watching the whole time but didn't think it was necessary to say I had spent about ten minutes inside Kathy's house, otherwise occupied.

The officer turned to go back to the Malloy house. The other officer used Dean's key to unlock the front door and enter the house. "Wait here," he told Dean. Entering, he called out, "Police!" The second officer went in after him.

After only a few minutes inside, one of the officers came back onto the porch alone, talking into the microphone attached at his shoulder. He said something quietly to Dean. Dean broke down crying and screaming uncontrollably.

"No, no, it can't be!" He dropped to his knees, his shoulders shook with every sob. "Why would she do that? It doesn't make any sense!"

Goose bumps raised on my arms and up my neck. I knew something terrible must have happened.

I looked at Kathy and couldn't help but see the fear and confusion in her eyes. She hopped up and ran inside to wake Bill. He and Dean were as close as brothers. If something bad really had happened, Dean would need Bill. When they came out of their house, Kathy and Bill rushed across the street.

I stood on their porch and stared in disbelief as they got to Dean and heard the horrific news ... Jessie had killed herself in the bathtub. While we were sitting on the porch drinking wine, our neighbor took her own life.

The next several hours were a blur of flashing lights and people bustling around doing their jobs ... police officers, crime scene techs, the coroner, and reporters. Everyone wanted to ask us questions, get our statements, pry into Jessie and Dean's private lives, and elicit our opinions on how something so dreadful could happen in a quiet neighborhood this.

By the time the sun came up, I was physically and emotionally exhausted. I called my boss and explained what had happened. She was very considerate and let me have the day off. I slept through the morning.

The doorbell rang, and I went to answer it.

"I'm Detective Anderson," the man said. He had his badge and ID in his right hand. "Are you Lisa Miller?"

"Yes, I am."

"I need to ask you some more questions about what happened last night." He sounded almost apologetic. "I want you to accompany me downtown to the station."

"But I already answered your officers' question," I said. "I'm not sure what else I can tell you."

"I'm sorry, but I must insist you come with me."

Now I understood why he had that tone. He was going to inconvenience me, and he knew I wouldn't be happy about it.

"Okay, but at least let me put on some decent clothes and brush my hair."

"Of course, but make it quick."

I went upstairs to change, wondering what I had become part of. *The police told Dean that Jessie had committed suicide. Why all this?*

The questioning lasted several hours. The questions ran the gamut of the last four months. The detectives wanted to know everything I had witnessed or heard about Jessie and Dean Malloy, Kathy and Bill Jenkins and other neighbors. The police were particularly interested in my interactions with Jessie and Dean, separately and as a couple. They even asked me why I bought this specific house. It was a grueling ordeal.

* * *

When I got home from work on Thursday around six o'clock, I could barely get into my driveway. Police cars and crime scene vehicles were parked all around the cul-de-sac. I heard people shouting in my back yard. *What in the world is going on out there?*

I went inside and straight to the kitchen. Peering out the window, I could see yellow crime scene tape strung around tree trunks and branches all long the back of the Malloy's house, my house, and the one next door.

"I've got all the pictures I need," someone called out.

"Done with casts of the footprints," another announced.

I watched for a few minutes as the technicians collected and bagged everything of interest for transport back to the lab. When they were finished, they packed up all their equipment. One by one the vehicles drove away. The yellow tape was the only evidence left behind to say they were there.

I wonder what they were looking for out there? I wonder if they found it?

* * *

Dean made all the arrangements for the visitation on Sunday evening and the funeral on Monday morning. I went to the visitation and expressed my condolences to him and Jessie's family, but I didn't feel right taking time off work to go to the funeral. I had only known Jessie for a short time.

Kathy and I spent several evenings after the funeral speculating why the police were still investigating a suicide. The lead detective wasn't ready to close the book on it and officially declare it a suicide. Evidently, something was nagging him. Some loose end, some box that needed to be check.

One evening, we were sitting on the deck near my pool, but my mind was elsewhere.

"Did something happen at work today?" Kathy asked. "You seem out of sorts tonight."

"Sorry. I guess I'm a little concerned about a letter I got today from my security company. When the police questioned me, I told them about the system I had installed. Apparently the police requested all my security videos from the past several months. The company turned them over, but they wanted me to know." I shrugged my shoulders. "Guess there's nothing I can do about it now."

"When did you get a security system installed?"

"About a month after I moved in. When I was looking at buying the house, I discussed the safety of having a pool with the real estate agent. I also raised it with my insurance broker.

Marty, my insurance guy, said I could get a discount on my premium if I installed a whole house security system with a video camera pointed at the pool. That way I'd have proof that I was following the rules in the event anyone ever injured themselves, or worse, drowned in my pool.

Marty said people like to sue homeowners with pools. They're easy pickings if they don't have proof of what really happened. You know, my word against theirs. He recommended a guy who came out and put the system in. It only took about twenty minutes. The camera is motion-activated. The video feeds directly to the security company, so I don't have to do anything except pay the monthly bill."

Kathy looked at my house and the roof line until she spotted the tiny camera in the corner. It was barely visible in the eave of the roof. If you didn't know to look for it, you wouldn't even notice it.

"How come you never mentioned it to us? I mean we were out here a lot this summer. I never knew we were being filmed."

"Well, for one, my broker suggested it would be better if no one knew. He even told me not to put out one of those signs telling everyone that passes by that I have a security system. He said it would do its best work if no one paid any attention to it. Secondly, I guess I never thought it would be an issue." I paused to gage Kathy's reaction. "I surely never thought the police would need to see the videos."

Kathy glanced back up at the camera. "I wonder what they saw on those tapes. Must be something interesting for them to still be investigating. I wish they'd just call it a suicide, so we can get back to normal around here."

"Yeah, me too." I looked out past the pool in the direction the camera pointed to see what it could have possibly picked up that would interest the police. Nothing out there but the back half of my yard and the partially overgrown area between my back yard and the adjoining neighborhood's backyards. And a few remnants of the yellow crime scene tape fluttering in the breeze.

* * *

I was about to sit down to dinner one evening in early August when I saw flashing lights and heard tires squealing to a halt outside. I stepped out on the porch as another police car pulled up in front of Dean's house. Wearing bulletproof vests with guns drawn, the officers surrounded his house like he was some kind of hardened criminal who'd just robbed a bank. One officer told me to get inside my house immediately and stay away from the windows facing the Malloy house.

Of course, that's like telling a child not to eat cookies before dinner. The first thing they do is head for the cookie jar. Peering out the side window, I saw them lead Dean out of the house, his hands in cuffs behind his back. They put him into the back of a squad car, and everyone drove off in a parade of lights and sirens.

Rumors swirled around the neighborhood. Everyone had their own speculations. Someone said Jessie was obviously unstable and had attempted suicide several times before finally succeeding. Another neighbor said Dean was a wife beater and had gone too far that night and had killed her.

I had heard that Dean had cheated on Jessie, but now they were saying Jessie had also cheated on Dean. It was hard to know who or what to believe.

We were all shocked when we finally heard the news. The police charged Dean with first degree murder. They accused him of killing Jessie and staging it to look like a suicide.

How could that be? He wasn't even home when she died. Kathy and I both saw her go back into the house after Dean drove away. She was alive and well. And when he came back with the police, he didn't even go into the house, the police did. They were the ones who found her body and told Dean she was dead. *How could he have killed her?*

* * *

The District Attorney, William Morris, interviewed me twice in preparation for the trial once he decided he wanted me to testify. He thought the defense team would call me as a witness, because I had been outside watching the house with Kathy Jenkins. When they issued their witness list and my name wasn't on it, he called me in.

Miss Crawford, who handled most of the questioning during the prep sessions, warned me about the cross-examination. "The defense attorney could ask you about other things. Just answer every question, no matter who asks it, in a polite and positive manner." She patted my hand and added, "I'm sure you'll do fine."

The defense team issued a subpoena for Kathy to testify. I figured Kathy would get one. She had known Jessie and Dean longer and had first-hand knowledge of their marital misadventures and 'spats.' Because Kathy and I were testifying for different sides, the DA didn't want us to sit around for months comparing notes.

"If you stay away from each other between now and the trial, the defense attorney won't be able to impugn your testimony by claiming collusion," the DA explained. What he didn't explain was that not speaking to each other for the next several months would, in effect, kill our budding friendship. *An unexpected casualty in this ordeal.*

He advised me not to talk to her husband or any of the other neighbors. "Any friendly conversations," he said, "will eventually lead to a discussion about the trial and we can't have that."

* * *

In the months that followed, I saw a few news reports about the case. The one report confirmed the existence of videos the district attorney claimed would play a key part in the case, but the DA kept the specific details hush-hush.

Another report said the police had uncovered a garbage bag full of wet clothes buried in the brush between the houses on our street and the neighboring one. That was the exact same area the police had searched after the incident. The report went on to say the clothing had traces of Dean's DNA and Jessie's blood. Neither the police nor the DA's office would confirm those reports.

The trial date finally rolled around in March of the next year. Kathy and I found ourselves sitting on a bench in the same hallway, waiting for someone from our respective legal teams to tell us where to go. We looked at each other as if we were strangers. Although we'd seen each other in passing in the neighborhood, our daily visits had ended long ago.

Because we were both witnesses, we had to be available when called, but we could not sit in the courtroom. They did not allow us to listen to any of the trial because it might influence our testimony.

Miss Crawford finally appeared and led me to a conference room away from prying eyes and reporters. "You'll be safe I here." She pointed to the pitcher of water and glasses in the center of the table. "Help yourself." With that, she left, and I was alone.

I sat down at one end of the long table. *This is going to be a long week. I wonder how long it will take the prosecution to present their case.*

Miss Crawford had said earlier that they might get to me by the third day, but most likely it would be on the fourth. A friend who's a legal secretary warned me that with lawyers, *everything* takes longer than it should.

I asked if I had to be there the whole time or if I could just show up on the day they needed me on the witness stand. Mr. Morris said I had to be there in case he needed to call me out of order. I couldn't imagine what would cause that to happen, but I'd never been a witness in a murder trial before now.

The days creeped along. While I waited, I read a Laura Childs book I'd been trying to find time to read. I'd picked up her first and second books, *Keepsake Crimes* and *Photo Finished,* a few years ago at a yard sale, thinking they sounded interesting. I had finished the first one quickly, but never got around to reading the second one. I figured this was my opportunity. About halfway through the second book, the door opened and Miss Crawford poked her head in. "Mrs. Miller, they're ready for you now."

I stuffed the book into my oversized purse, left the book and purse in the witness room, and followed her to the courtroom.

"State your full name for the record." The bailiff said

"Lisa Mae Miller."

"Raise your right hand."

Standing in the witness box, I did as commanded. I listened intently to the words the bailiff recited.

"Do you solemnly swear to tell the truth, the whole truth and nothing but the truth, under pains and penalties of perjury?"

Solemnly swear ... the whole truth ... pains and penalties. The words echoed in my brain. *This is surreal.*

"I do." Those two spoken words immediately reminded me of another solemn occasion when I had uttered them. *Oh, how I missed Harry.*

"Please sit." The bailiff's gruff tone snapped me back to the present reality.

Mr. Morris approached the witness box and, dispensing with all pleasantries, asked his first question. "Mrs. Miller, do you live in the house next door to the defendant?"

Is that a little bit of hostility in his tone? "Yes, my house is on the left if you're facing it from the street."

"Just answer the questions I ask, ma'am." He looked at the jury, then back at me. "How long had you lived there before the night of July 19th?"

"About four months."

"Did you know anyone in the neighborhood before you bought the house and moved in?"

"No."

"And, in the four months after moving in, you'd gotten to know your neighbors, particularly Jessie and Dean Malloy.?"

"Yes."

"Would you say you were friendly with them?"

There was definitely some hostility in his voice. *I wonder why he's taking an attitude with me. This was not going at all like we had practiced it during the prep sessions.*

"Well, yes, I was friendly with them, mostly Jessie ... but I did speak to Dean when I saw him out in the yard."

Mr. Morris turned again towards the jury box and smirked.

Ah ha ... that explains his attitude against me. He's playing to the jury. It must be part of his strategy ... but to what end, I had no clue.

Still facing the jury, he said, "We've already heard testimony from the representative of your security company regarding the closed-circuit monitoring camera they installed in your back yard and the jury has seen the video recordings pertinent to this case. We need you to confirm a few details for the record."

He turned toward me. "Why did you decide to install the camera in your back yard?"

"It was my insurance agent's idea because of the pool. He said I could get a lower rate and it would provide protection in the event I was ever sued."

"Do you recall what day and time it was installed?"

"The appointment was on Thursday, April 28th at two o'clock in the afternoon. It took about twenty minutes to install."

"Do you recall if any of your neighbors were home on that afternoon?"

"I really wasn't paying too much attention, but I did notice that the Malloy's were both gone – at work, I assume. And the Jenkins' across the street were gone. Kathy and Bill were at work and their boys were in school."

The DA turned towards the jury again. "So, you had the security system, including the camera, installed on a work day when all your neighbors were gone, and you didn't post any signs saying you had surveillance on the premises. Did you ever tell anyone you had it installed ... specifically, prior to the night in question?"

"No, my agent advised me against advertising its presence, and I didn't think it was necessary to tell anyone."

"So, it's your testimony that you never discussed the presence of a surveillance camera in your back yard with any of your neighbors between the time it was installed in April and the night of July 19th, correct?

"Yes, that's correct."

"Your Honor, I have no further questions for this witness." The DA walked back to his chair and sat down. He looked quite pleased with his performance.

I held my breath as I waited for the defense attorney. He was whispering something into Dean's ear.

"The Defense has no questions for this witness."

The judge looked at me and announced, "The witness is excused."

A whoosh of trapped air escaped through my parted lips in a whistle that I was sure the jury could hear. The bailiff helped me exit the witness box and escorted me past the tables where Miss Crawford was standing. She escorted me out of the courtroom.

"The DA has a couple of more witnesses before he rests his side of the case. Then the defense will present their side. That will take a few more days at least. I don't know when we'll get to closing arguments, but for now, you're free to go."

"Do you think I'll be recalled to the stand?"

"No, Mr. Morris covered everything he wanted, and their side didn't even bother to ask any questions. They did not reserve the right to recall you, and I doubt they will. There was nothing they could refute with your testimony.

* * *

Time passed slowly in the days following my court appearance. I had gotten back into my normal routine at work when the phone rang. It was Miss Crawford.

"The closing arguments were this morning, and the jury started deliberating around one o'clock. We don't have any idea how long it will take, but the DA is confident they'll come back with a guilty verdict. We thought you might want to know, in case you hear something on the news either tonight or tomorrow."

"Thanks for the heads up. I appreciate the call." I knew it wasn't Mr. Morris' idea for her to call me, even though she used the royal "we."

As I was getting ready for bed that night, I turned on the news. Sure enough, the lead story was the verdict in the Malloy Murder Trial. The jury only took three hours to find Dean Malloy guilty of first degree murder. The verdict was unanimous. Dean's attorney argued that Jessie had killed herself and staged the scene to frame Dean for her "murder." The jury didn't see it that way.

One juror, interviewed by a news reporter after the verdict, said, "If we hadn't seen the backyard videos showing him scouting out the path between the houses on the moonlit nights in the two months preceding his wife's death, we probably would have bought his story."

"He'd obviously been planning it for a long time," another juror said. "The hidden camera and the surprise rain shower were his undoing."

I pushed the off button on the TV remote and settled into bed.

I wonder what would have happened if I hadn't bought this house when I did.

NAME YOUR POISON

By *Leslie Bush*

1

Standing at my laboratory table in the dark recesses of my room, I mixed together the ingredients of the formula. With some satisfaction, I watched the particles settle lazily to the bottom. I clicked the container with my bone finger, causing an ominous chime from the glass. A green puff of vile smoke rose outward. I knew the potion was complete.

Turning to Tallon, the young man, who sat uncomfortably in the wooden chair in another dark corner of my room, I wished I had the lips to leer at him, but the visage of grinning death that my undead face conveyed should have been enough. The dim candlelight played across his ashen face like unsettled spirits, looking for a victim to drain of life. Being an undead wizard, I had no need for any light, and I certainly kept no light for the convenience of company. The dancing flames cast the eerie shadows that leant well to the image I wished to project upon my victim.

"I should let the rot take you," I growled, as I handed him the potion.

He shifted his weight uncomfortably "But you won't, Mal."

"Do not call me 'Mal'! You know bloody well my name is Malhavoc! I will not tolerate any shortening of my name!"

He did not argue, as he took the offering from my bone hand. The vapors enwrapped his face for a moment to create a glowing green aura around him. He only shrugged and held his nose, as he gulped the drink down. Suddenly, his face turned a startling shade of purple, then he coughed violently. Finally, he spat, and his face, turned back to a normal, healthy color to my dismay. If he had died, I could have always claimed that it was a miscalculation and not my fault. Catching his breath, he glared at me. I would have smiled, if I still had lips.

"What on Amgen did you put in that potion, Mal?"

I only looked at him. It did no good correcting him on my name.

"Curdled bat toenails?"

"It was more like festered innards of a toad."

"The goal is not to kill me, you know!"

I made the flames of my magically induced eyes burn fiercer. "I am an undead necromancer! My job is not to cure idiots like you, who mess around with the zombie prostitutes! My special job is to create zombies!"

"Yeah. Yeah. You keep making potions like that one, and you'll put Jeriah out of business!"

"I have no interest in Jeriah's business!" Crossing my arms, I cocked my head. "Since when did I become your healer?"

"Since Nikodemus, my glorious master, pays your fee to stay here at the tower."

"Get out of my room!" I cried out, clenching my fists. My flames for my eyes burned fiercer.

"Yeah, yeah," he replied, as he jumped out of the chair. "I'm going to go visit the esteemed Jeriah. Want to join me? It might be fun. I'm certain he can whip up something that might intrigue your tastes."

With an effort, I projected a calm I did not feel. "What use do I have for mind numbing drinks?"

"Who knows? There has to be some fun still left in those undead bones of yours, or else you wouldn't still be in this world."

"Get out!"

Tallon threw me a quick salute and scurried out of my room before I lost control and blasted him. It was for the best. He would have only dodged it, and I would have destroyed some of the precious books here.

With a curse, I threw up my hands and returned to my desk and the tome I was studying.

2

Once the nuisance of Tallon was gone from my presence, I settled down to my work again. I soon found a fascinating spell that I could accommodate to my use. Rubbing my hands together, I was most eager to try this out on a deserving victim. With my special talents, the death throes would be spectacular and could last after death. I only needed the proper test subject.

Tallon ran into my laboratory again. Any other time I would complain about the lack of effectiveness of my barrier spells, but this was a sign of fate. I cracked my knuckles and wondered how I could make this man's destruction look like an accident. Then again, once the spell was done with him, there would only be fine bits of blood, bone, and gore happily splattered into the mortar of the far wall. No one would be the wiser.

Although the fantasy was most pleasing, I knew better. Nikodemus was too good of a wizard not to trace the remnants of his apprentice and the spell that obliterated him. I had far too much research to do here to be exiled from the tower and its library. I was quite a powerful wizard, proof by my state of being, but Nikodemus was much more powerful. Someday, I would surpass him and destroy him and everything that he held dear.

Without any hesitation, Tallon grabbed hold of my arms. "Mal! You've got to help! It's terrible!"
Pulling my arms away from him, I had to wonder at the lack of fear these fools had of the visage of Death. When I was a child in Kruskusa, the people there were averse to touching anything dead. Apparently, this was not the case in Portstown. Regardless, I looked up at his face.

Tallon was far too tall for his own good. I was certain that if I tried hard enough, I could find a spell to shrink him down to a more reasonable size. Of course, it would be more fun to cut off his legs.

"Go away! You have disturbed my studies enough!"

"Oh, come on," he pleaded. "You're the best necromancer in town, and only you can help!"

"I am the only necromancer you can exploit."

"Well. Yes. I guess you have a point there. All the same, Jeriah is in trouble!"

"It serves him right. He should be more careful who he robs, yes?"

"You don't understand. The Purple Unicorn is being haunted by a vile ghost."

"Since when has that bothered anyone?" In all of Amgen, Portstown was the most accepting of the undead. Vampires hunted the night. Zombies shambled into the streets. Ghouls prowled the graveyards. Ghosts haunted the woodwork. As far as I could tell, I was the only lich in town. No one treated me any different than anyone else. I have never encountered such a group of idiots, who had no clue what dangers the undead posed.

Tallon threw out his arms in a dramatic pose. "It's not like Jeriah cares if they have a pulse or not. They're welcome there as long as they pay. This ghost is different. He is stealing all the alcohol out of the drinks!"

"Is there anything left?" I asked sarcastically.

"Listen, Mal! We can taste exactly how bad the drinks are now! If we can't get drunk, then Jeriah will lose his business! What will become of Portstown?"

"It will be a much better place without that sleaze hole and its rodent owner! You might stay sober long enough to become a true wizard instead of a slacker of an apprentice," I answered as I returned to my books.

"Jeriah likes you. He doesn't give just anyone an everlasting tab."

Gritting my teeth, I slowly put my pen down. Purposely, I turned on Tallon. "Do I look like I need food or drink? I am a walking skeleton!"

"You never know. One of those mind-blowing drinks might do you a world of good."

"I do not have a throat to swallow such poisons."

Standing up straight, Tallon scratched the back of his head. "Yeah. You do have a point there."

I shook my head and gave up on my present work for the time. I gathered the books I was done researching. Since this fool would not allow me to study, I would take the opportunity to return some of the books to the library. Taking up my seven-foot-long, bone staff, I swung it at Tallon. Unfortunately, he was limber enough to avoid contact with it. Having the unnatural strength of the undead, I could give some serious impact with such a swing. Of course, I could harm him with just a mere touch from it. I had acquired the staff when I defeated my master Emeirikol, and like its previous owner (and present one), it did not like beings who were not of an evil nature. Of course, I would have liked it a couple of feet shorter. The bloody thing made me look like a pixie!

Ignoring my threat, Tallon followed me. "What do you say? You could charge the amount of your fee," he suggested.

"Getting a gold coin from Jeriah is worse than getting a copper button from a dragon. I cannot imagine getting fifteen pounds of gold from him."

"He would owe you greatly for this. I'm certain that he would do it."

"I have better things to do with my time."

"Come on, Mal!" he begged, as he knelt before me and grabbed my robes. "Please!"

I should be like other liches and blast him with the cold of the Netherworld. Shaking my head, I pulled my robe free. Such spells shot back a cold with them. I hated cold almost as much as I did rats.

Reaching the double doors of the library, I felt an uncanny tremble run up my spine. If I were still alive, a cold sweat would have burst from my pores. Being what I was, I could only feel that ache in my bones.

I shook my head, as I pulled the doors open. I should have learned over the centuries not to ignore such feelings. A wave of loud disharmonic noise, followed by a pungent stench, washed over me.

> Sitting here all alone,
> My gracious audience fled for Redemption Road,
> 'Cause of nasty bogeys and their boogers!
> Oh Jim, Jimi, and Jimmy,
> Did you ever suffer such horrible narcs?
> But, it's great to have buds in the bud!
> Whoa! Old Nicky Man!
> You saved my bacon, and my weed, and my 'shrooms, too.
> You're way cool, dude
> But you need more groovy groupies in your group!

"What in the bloody Abyss is that blasted bard doing in the tower?" I demanded loudly, as I pointed a shaking finger at the invading being.

In the center of the library and on top of one of the tables, the blue haired, half elf known as Kel, danced around with a battered guitar. Overly bright colors were swirled around his shirt and pants, as if he had been in a brutal battle with varying berry bushes. He lost this fight, of course. His hemp pants were ragged and torn in several spots, because he had the terrible tendency of ripping off strips of it and smoking it, when he ran out of his vile tobacco or magic mushrooms. Speaking of which, the whole library hung heavy with the smoke and the stench.

"Oh, he is just staying here until the ghost situation is taken care of at the Unicorn. His mushrooms and tobacco have no effects on him there because of this ghost," Nikodemus said, as he came up from behind me.

The master of the tower was a dark-skinned elf-pixie with dark hair and eyes. He wore a simple yellow shirt with a black dot in one corner, a black slash in another corner, and a red tongue in the middle of it. Fortunately, his hemp pants were whole. His only redeeming quality was that he was a good foot shorter than me.

"Wow!" exclaimed Kel, as he bounded towards us. "The acoustics in this place are fantastic!"

Shifting my staff to my right hand, I moved my left to cast a spell that would obliterate this blue haired atrocity.

"Ack!" Nikodemus pushed my hand down. "Now, none of that, old boy. Remember rule number three. No killing."

"Unless in self-defense. I am trying to protect my sanity!"

"Tsk! Tsk! We all know better. That temper of yours will get the better of you yet."

"Yeah, Grateful Dead Dude," Kel told me, as he handed me a mushroom. "Chill, man. Have a mushroom suppository. They're great, you just shove them up your … "

I forced the flames of my eyes to burn fiercer. "No one should treat a lich like this! I should lay waste to this tower and everyone in it!"

"But you won't. That would be a great loss of knowledge that you don't have, and if you kill me, who will pay your weight in gold to the dragon?" Nikodemus said.

My hand tightened around my staff, and I ground my teeth. Through a series of terrible circumstances, I became the property of Skratch the dragon. I had sold my soul to a demon when I was alive, and the demon gave my soul to Skratch for services rendered. In essence, it was my just deserves for dealing with such untrustworthy allies.

Fortunately, I was nothing but bones, and I weighed fifteen pounds with the heavy outfit I wore at the time of weighing. Every month, Nikodemus paid Skratch my weight in gold, so that he could use my services. Mostly, Nikodemus wanted me to share my research with him and Tallon. The two of them did likewise with me, not that I really studied their kind of magic.

"I will pay my own way!" I announced. "I will get rid of that bloody ghost! Then you can send that vile creature back to the hellhole from which he came!"

Kel threw his arms around me, making me lose my staff and books in the process. "Thank you so much, Grateful Dead Dude! I so need to get back to my mushroom garden and do some weeding! How will I ever repay you? I know! I'll write the grooviest of songs in your honor!"

"Good show, old fellow! I knew you were up to the task," Nikodemus happily stated, as he slapped hands with Tallon.

I had been duped again. My shoulders dropped in defeat. I truly hated them. Picking up my staff and books, I swore someday I would destroy this wizard and his apprentice. I would delight in enslaving their souls to my will for eternity. For now, I would be their patsy and do their work.

3

Teleportation was my main mode of travel. Being a wizard for almost all of my existence, teleportation was more normal for me than walking. Unfortunately, this kind of magic did not work within the tower. Unlike most of the restrictions placed on my actions, this was not one of Nikodemus' asinine rules, but the very nature of the place. The tower was within a dimension within itself or all dimensions at once. I have yet to discover the answer. Access to all worlds was possible through the tower and through a place called the Hall of Doors. An infinite number of doors lined each side of this room, and all leading to a different place. Nikodemus, Tallon and Kel explored these doorways. This was the reason why Kel had such an odd fashion sense and dialect. He was quite fond of a hellish place called Woodstock, where peace, love and weed was the law. Yes. I had been around the idiot too long, and I knew too much about him and his philosophy. I would vomit if I still had a stomach.

Having only been here for a few weeks, I was unsure which door led where. I had spent most of my time in the library and my laboratory. The Dead were not meant for travel, especially my kind of undead. Liches were scholarly types, and I was no different from my ilk in this. All the same, on this day it would have been useful to know which doors led to different parts of Amgen and specifically Portstown.

Heavy breathing made me turn around. Tallon stopped in front of me. He bent over and grasped his legs. Once he caught his breath, he stood up straight before me. Yeah. I preferred to see him bent over in pain, but all delights must end.

"Thought you might need some help along the way," he told me.

"My soul will be frozen and gnawed on by rats in the deepest pits of Hell before I need the help of a half-cocked apprentice."

"That might be so, old fellow, but I do know the doors. I have been here a bit longer than you have," he replied without contempt.

I crossed my arms. "The cockroaches have been here longer than I have been."

Ignoring my comment, he made his way to a door. He motioned for me to follow. I dropped my shoulders in defeat. I guess I could accept his help this once. When I teleported with the use of the power around me, I knew what to expect, but this was something completely different. I was at the mercy of the power of the doorways. When Tallon and I went through the door, we appeared in the streets of Portstown, and I unceremoniously fell into him.

"Quite a ride, isn't it, old fellow?" he remarked, as he caught my falling body.

Any other time, I would be inclined to hit him with my staff. Instead, I balanced it away from him. It would not do for him to drop me before I regained my equilibrium. Once firmly on my feet, I pulled away from him and took in my surroundings.

I was a skeletal wizard, who did not deal in illusions. I made no attempt to disguise what I was. I was proud of what I had done to myself, and one of my greatest desires was for the ordinary person to look upon me and flee, screaming in terror. I never had that good of fortune.

The people of Portstown walked by us as if we were nothing out of the ordinary. A few of them even hailed us . . . especially me in a friendly voice.

I took several stumbling steps backwards. With a hasty movement of my hand, I cast the spell that would teleport me to the Purple Unicorn instantly. Yes. Unfortunately, I had visited this filthy dive before now. That was the way of teleportation spells. I could only use the spell to go to places that held the signature of my presence, and I had been to the Purple Unicorn three times before now. None of these times had I been there by my own choice. The first time was for the demon's task. I had to find a book that Jeriah had stolen. The second time was at Skratch's bidding. The last time was Nikodemus' idea and the payment for losing the duel against him. The best thing about this spell was that Tallon had not mastered it yet. I would lose his company for a while.

A name such as "The Purple Unicorn" brought to mind the idea of cute, little pink fairies, puffy dandelions, and a pastel purple horse with a horn. Such was not the feel here. Yes, there was a picture of a unicorn with a purple face. He sat back on his haunches and cried out in pain. Little red lightning bolts came from his hidden genitals. It did my soul good to see such a pure animal in so much pain.

The Purple Unicorn was the only tavern in town. If it were not, I was certain that it would do no business at all. The food was rancid, and the entertainment was worse. Granted, I no longer had the need to eat, but food, slopped in an indiscernible green and brown mass on a plate cannot be appetizing, especially when it bit back. As for the entertainment, Kel was the main attraction. Enough said there. The main reason people came here was for Jeriah's special drinks. He even catered to some of the more specialized tastes as well. I have no need of drink either, but I had seen the results of these volatile potions. I would never understand why sentient beings would want to be insensible, but that was what brought the citizens of Portstown into this establishment.

The dive was blissfully quiet for a change. After all, the musical entertainment was elsewhere. Evening was coming on by this time, and the interior took on its darkness. Looking around the tavern in this gloom, I felt the place may be tolerable.

Kelly, the well-endowed half elf barmaid sat at one of the shaded booths. Her pale shapely face was ghost-like in the lantern light. Her long red hair was tied back, and she propped up her feet on the opposite chair. She fixed her blue eyes on her task. She was doing her nails.

At another table sat one of the two patrons in the place at this time. He was the sturdy, grizzled dwarf known as Bloodstone. Dwarves were known to be a burly bunch, and cleanliness was not one of their top priorities, but Bloodstone was an exceptional piece. He put filthy vagabonds to shame. I doubted that he ever removed his clothes, and I had firsthand experience with the removal of his boots. Things withered and died from those gaseous emissions. I might well have gleaned the reason why these people had no fear of me.

Behind him stood the other patron. The imposing seven-foot-tall figure of a minotaur was enough to intimidate the stoutest of hearts. Minotaurs were known throughout all dimensions for their fierceness and battle rage. The great head of the bull with its massive horns could inflict some impressive damage even upon a dragon. On one of his massive biceps was a tattoo of a heart with the word "Moo." Yeah, but this was Taurus, and he and Bloodstone were the proud owners of the local dairy farm. I was not sure I wanted to know the meaning behind that one.

Across from these two, crouched the equally odorous creature known as Maxwell, the Unicorn's kobold cook. He looked much like a three-foot-tall rat terrier on its hind legs. An expressive rat tail wagged behind him. Maxwell smelled like a dog that had rolled in cow manure, died, and laid out in the hot sun for six days. Max prided himself upon the fact that he could make a meal out of any available material. Being a subspecies of goblins, he could stomach just about anything. The patrons of the Unicorn found a better use for the vile substance. They would purchase his putrid dishes to throw at the musical entertainment. Since Kel was at the tower, this cook was out of a job.

Bloodstone and Max were playing a game called Ships and Buckles. Neither one of them knew the slightest thing about either thing. That did not matter in these kinds of games. Nikodemus had spent some time in teaching me the rules and the techniques of the game. Since it had nothing to do with bloody dismemberment, I would have been better off with the book *Necrotic Diseases of Necromantic Autopsies*. Regardless, I knew the rules of the game.

It was more of a game of chance than anything. Max flipped a pair of dice into a bowl on the table with a spoon. If the dice landed in the bowl and the bowl stayed on the table, he won the round. If the dice landed on an odd number, it was twice as valuable. For a goblin, Max was good. The dice landed square in the bowl; one was a three, the other a four.

To best his opponent, Bloodstone would have to throw a seven or better odd in the bowl. The dwarf grumbled some entertaining curses and took up the dice. Chewing on his ratty beard, he loaded the spoon. He pulled back on the spoon, squinted his right eye, and took aim at the bowl.

"By the mug of Althgar!" he swore, as he let go the shot.

Just as his fingers let go of the spoon, he let go a tremendous belch. The dice went flying. Max ducked the missile with the expert skills that he had acquired from years of practice.

Taurus exclaimed a "Moo!" as he dodged the other die.

Once the dust settled, Max jumped up on the table. "I won! Hand over the cheese!"

"@#$% kobold!" cried out Bloodstone.

With a few more entertaining dwarven words, Bloodstone dug into his filthy clothes and produced a lump of mold that may have been cheese at one time. The stench of the substance washed over me as I stood by the door. I had smelt decayed corpses that had less of a stench. Kelly casually pulled a handkerchief from her bodice and covered her mouth and nose with it like a bandit. Without hesitation, she returned to her nails.

"Moo!" coughed Taurus, as he turned away from the table.

Max snatched the cheese from Bloodstone's hand. He gave it a long, loving sniff and yelped happily. Without hesitation, he popped it into his mouth. Perhaps, he was more goblin than I gave him credit for.

Bloodstone clenched his fists and glared at Max. "Someday, I'm gonna string you up by that cheating rat tail of yours, you filthy dog!"

"Moo snuffle growl moo moo," Taurus complained.

"Ack! What do you know about the rules of the game! Of course, he's cheating! How else do you think he's won all them games in a row!" Bloodstone blurted back at him, as he pulled a flask out of his pants.

Taurus only shook his great bullhead.

Bloodstone took a swig from the flask. A sour expression crossed his face. His jaw puffed out, and he spat the contents across the table. The spit hit Max, knocking him off the table.

The kobold jumped back up on the chair. Looking down at his splattered clothes, he spread a wide smile. He turned back to the dwarf. "Why thank you, Bloodstone! And I thought you mad at me for beating you!"

"Jeriah!" Bloodstone cried out, ignoring Max. "You've gotta get rid of that accursed ghost! My brew tastes as bad as a cow's ass!"

"Shut up and pay your bill, you lousy flea infested dwarf!" yelled back Jeriah, as he emerged from the back room.

Jeriah was a round rodent of a man. He had dark, beady eyes, and a too large mouth that cut into his fur covered, fat cheeks. His arms and legs were too short for his body, but he was still taller than me by a few inches. Yet his hands had long, nimble fingers that could pick pockets with great precision.

He turned his dark eyes towards me. A chill ran down my spine. With an effort, I remained in place instead of fleeing. Things only got worse for me. He ran to me and embraced me tightly. Gritting my teeth, I did my best to keep my composure and not incinerate him. Although I could claim the action as self-defense, it would not solve the problem at the tower.

"Mal! You're finally here to take care of my ghost problem!" he exclaimed.

"Uhm, yes," I replied, as I pried myself out of his embrace. My staff may be a formidable weapon against those in the tower, but this vile tavern keeper was unaffected by its touch, as it brushed him. "For a price, of course."

"Of course! Of course! My good man . . . skeleton . . . whatever," he replied with that devious, buck tooth grin that reminded me of a large rat with an abandoned infant. The ice ran down my back several degrees colder. Clenching my fists, I reminded myself that I had to do business with this man. "You already have free food and drink here. Perhaps, you would like a free pass to the entertainment here."

Shifting my jaw, I kept visual contact with him and did not move to smite him. "The entertainment of this sleaze hole is the reason I am here. You can have him back. I want real payment."

"Alright, if you get rid of the ghost then you can have the first bid on the corpses of the customers who are foolhardy enough to eat Max's cooking. A fresh corpse is always a necromancer's delight.," he offered with a wink. "And I do get a few women through here."

"I do not need your clientele. I can get dead bodies anywhere and of my own making. I had something more valuable in mind."

"Well, yeah, I would give you my soul, but you've got to wait in line for that one."

Sometimes I thought these fools did not understand the nature of my business. After all, when I told him that I did necromancy, one of Tallon's friends wanted me to introduce him to my great friends Ned and Nancy. The longer I stayed in this ridiculous town, the more I realized they did indeed understand. They just did not care. The Bloody Abyss! This took all the fun out of my work!

"I want fifteen pounds of gold from that heap of yours."

"What! Bleed me dry, will you! What kind of price is that? You know gold is the life's blood of the Unicorn, you vampire!"

"And here I thought it was that caustic acid you call liquor. If my price is too high, I will take my business elsewhere."

"No! No! I'll pay. I need to get rid of this pest and now!"

Any other business, this price would be an absorbent amount, but Jeriah could afford it. He not only made foul brews, kept an unpaid staff, had some shady deals on the side, but he was a lowlife thief. An intelligent person would stay out of this place, but if he had to come here, he entered the establishment with only the pay needed for the services rendered. If he brought anything extra here, the customer would not leave with it. Jeriah prided himself on those potent drinks, and an unconscious customer was a healthy tip for Jeriah and his staff. The victim was picked cleaner than a corpse was by ravenous raccoons.

Grumbling, the man left the room. I heard another vile curse, but I was not particularly on guard. I was unsure if it came from Jeriah or Bloodstone, who still played the game of chance. After a quarter of an hour, Jeriah returned with a sack in his hands. Squinting his eyes at me, he held the sack close to his heart like a child.

"You'd better do this right, necromancer, or I'll feed your first-born child to the rats of Shady Valley."

He was a bit late for that one. Giving the sack a final loving caress, he whispered parting words to it. He closed his eyes and turned his back as he held the sack out to me. I wrapped my skeletal fingers around it. With a small exertion of my strength, I pulled it away from him.

Knowing Jeriah as I did, I cast a spell on the contents to assure myself that it was what it was supposed to be. It would not surprise me if he gave me a bag of gold painted rat pellets. With a nod, I had the confirmation of the spell. The gold was indeed gold and the amount I asked. The man had to be truly desperate to give into my price so easily. I cast another spell that put the gold into a storage dimension that I kept.

With everything in place, I grasped my staff with both hands and prepared to do my work.

4

Hitting the floor with my staff, I cast the spell. A resounding boom and a tremor shook the structure. Unfortunately, the Purple Unicorn was a strong enough structure to withstand the strain. Reality shimmered around me and the other occupants. I stood back and surveyed the results.

I shook my head and had to wonder about the wisdom of using this spell. The World of the Living overlapped with Limbo, enabling all to see those who haunted this place. Yeah, I got more than I bargained for. The place was more crowded than on the nights that Kel was not there, and Kelly did her belly-dance performance, or so Gallon told me. With a snap of my bone fingers, I filtered in only the strongest ghosts and dispelled the rest of them to a level of Limbo unseen.

Ghosts come in many varieties depending upon their strength and purpose. The stronger the ghost, the better they can interact with the Living World. Often, the strongest of these ghosts died in a violent way and sought vengeance. Hatred was a wonderfully powerful emotion. If the hate was intense enough, the ghost became a revenant or a wraith and could wreak some major havoc. Looking around at this lot, I knew I was in the wrong place for such entertainment.

All the same, there was a vast variety of spooks here, and all the useless kind one would expect from such an establishment. Several ghosts ran around the rafters. Cocking my head, I could detect a couple of poltergeists among them.

Poltergeists were mischievous spirits, who dwelt in Limbo, but they were never living beings. I was more than happy to expel such vermin, especially since they were rather rodent like. I was not paid to do such a job here at this time. They were running around with the other ghosts. They were playing some kind of ball game. A smaller ghost was the ball, being kicked around.

Another set of ghosts were sawing at the stage legs. What a delightful thought! Kel would return to the stage, and it would collapse with him. Maybe a sizeable shard would impale him and add some well-needed red to his colorful clothes. Alas, the ghosts were not substantial enough to affect this world.

In a corner was a ghost of a prostitute selling her wares. I would have to keep Tallon away from this one, or else I would have to brew that potion to resolve ethereal poisons. Another set of ghosts were playing cards at a table. Under the table, there were more poltergeists. Each of the poltergeists were handing the players cards from under the table. There was even a ghost near Bloodstone and Max. This ghost was giving Bloodstone tips on how to flip the dice. Yeah, Bloodstone was more bull-headed than his companion was and would do things his own way.

A scream and a curse came from Kelly. My attention turned to her. A ghost stuck his face in her bosom. His hands caressed her bottom. Muffled lecherous laughter came from him. Kelly did what she normally did on such occasions. She gave firm precise kicks to the groin of her attacker, but such attacks had no effect.

Feeling quite generous this evening, I would be her valiant knight in black wizard robes. Blagh! The idea was completely disgusting! On the other hand, the ghost was more so. I tapped the ghost on the shoulder. Unlike the living, I could touch any ghost. Not only was I a necromancer, but I was undead. I stood on both sides of life. In a way, I was an exceptionally strong ghost, who possessed a physical body. The ghost turned his head and looked at me with hooded eyes.

"Get your own woman, wimp! Rosie's free and cheap. She's none too picky neither."

My fingers closed around his collar. With gritted teeth, I pulled him bodily from his perch. For my entire existence, people have looked down on me. I was not about to put up with it from a two-bit lecherous ghost.

"I give you a choice," I growled through my clenched teeth. "You can leave her be, or I will send you to the Backlands of Limbo, where you will never see anything remotely female again."

"Try and do it! I'm certain she would prefer me to you any day. Most women don't do miniatures, you know."

The fingers of my right hand dug deep into his spiritual flesh. Leaning my staff into my shoulder, I moved my left hand with the spell. I wanted to feel his expulsion with my own hand. Pulling the proper strands of magic, I shoved my hand into his face. I cast the spell. His spiritual substance weakened and dissolved. With a curse, he disappeared with a pop.

"Take that, you vile rat," I grumbled as I turned to resume my work here. I hoped his soul was headed to a nice deep pit of the Abyss, where he belonged.

"Thank you," Kelly said, as she kissed me on the cheek bone.

Standing there a moment, I watched her return to her business . . . her manicure. I touched my cheek. Did she not see me for what I was? With a reminder of what these people of Portstown were like, I knew she did. Throwing up my hands, I had work to do and no time to think about pretty women. Such things would get me in more trouble than the necromancy would.

Jeriah did what he did best. He ran around the tavern in a frenzy. "Eeh! Pay up for those drinks! Don't just loiter there! Buy something or get out! I've got a business to run, you know!"

Yeah. Scaring these people was out of the question. Shaking my head, I returned to my own business. Looking at each ghost in turn, I assessed their strength by their glow. None of them were exceptionally strong. My vision turned to a ghost of a man, who sat at the bar with a mug of drink. This one's glow was a bit stronger than the rest.

This spirit was a tall, thin man with a round, balding head. His long delicate fingers seemed proportionate to his arms, unlike Jeriah. He wore a simple merchant's outfit. His long sleeves were rolled up to his elbows. Suspenders held up his pants. He only gazed silently at the mug of drink before him instead of joining in with the revelry of the other ghosts.

"And you are?" I inquired, as I took the seat next to him.

His sharp, intelligent eyes turned to me, and laughter wracked his frame. "Jeriah must be desperate to hire a shrimp like you. Kind of small for a necromancer, aren't you?" he answered.

Crossing my arms and gritting my teeth, I got up from my seat and stood my full five foot nothing height. "Are you the ghost causing the ruckus with the liquor here?"

"And what if I am, pipsqueak?"

"I can give you the same choice as the lech. We can work together, or I can send you onward like I did him."

"Hmpf! You won't find me an easy target."

"I suspect that I will not. Yet, I do specialize in this kind of work. You have a reason for being here. Tell me your name and your purpose, and, perhaps, I may be able to help you."

Narrowing his eyes at me, he replied, "Unlike the idiots around here, I know what you are and what you are capable of. I will not willingly give you my name."

He was correct in his train of thought. A necromancer can do many things to a person once he knew the person's name. I could do more and most frightful things to one who is dead. Assessing this man, I would never have thought him to know so much. All the same, he was safe from my control. I had enough ignoramuses around me as it was. I only wanted his name for easier reference, and it might worm more information out of Jeriah in solving this problem. A pleasant thought crossed my mind. This ghost could want Jeriah crucified on the rafters, and the ghosts there could use his head for their new ball.

"Albert! Albert Berr!" Jeriah cried out with his arms wide. Yeah. Jeriah just solved that problem. "How you been, you old sod? Well, I guess it can't be too good since you're dead and all."

"Shut up, Jeriah!" he snapped.

"Albert will be sufficient," I said. "I did not want to call you just 'ghost.' I would attract more attention than I wish. Are you the one sapping the alcohol from the drinks?"

"I am guilty of destroying all mind-altering substances here," he replied flatly.

Cocking my head, I stroked my chin in thought. "Granted I do not think your work is a bad thing, but I thought you crocks liked the effects of alcohol in your drinks."

"I'm dead. The alcohol no longer has any effect on me. Not that I cared all that much for Jeriah's sludge. My own was vastly superior."

"Yeah! Prove it!" Jeriah spat back.

Albert stood up straight. "If I hadn't died so suddenly, I would have shown you up! I know better than drink that piss you call drink!"

"Hey! It was a peace offering. That was all. Was it my fault that you choked on it?" complained Jeriah.

"Drinks aren't supposed to be chunky! What was in that muck? Chunks of lizard?"

"It was actually one of Kel's frogs finely diced," Jeriah admitted.

"When I recovered from the experience, I went home, and my prize still blew up with me."

"Yeah, well. I can't help that. It was your own doing. Who puts kerosene in their drink? Of course, the explosion was amazing. Kel left to dance naked around the bonfires for a whole week afterwards."

I did not want to know!

Albert lurched for Jeriah's throat, but his spirit was not strong enough to make contact. His hands went through him. Jeriah only leaned back and laughed. Actual physical contact may have been impossible for him, but he could sling bodily fluids. Although I was all for bloodshed and an all-out fight, I had a job to do. Unfortunately, not only could I touch ghosts, they could reciprocate. Wiping the residual spit from my face, I had to make my move now. When Albert undid his suspenders, I grabbed hold of him. No one wanted that show, nor did I want to be caught in the crossfire of anymore bodily fluids.

"I understand," I told him. "You are seeking vengeance, yes? Jeriah's bloody demise, perhaps?"

Settling down, he looked me straight in the face. Relaxing, he returned to his chair. "Well, not exactly. My greatest dream was to show up this shyster. My liquor was far superior to his in potency and taste."

"Yeah! Prove it!" spat Jeriah.

"I can't! I'm dead! I can't touch anything!"

"And that's my fault?" Jeriah complained with a surprisingly straight face.

"Hold your tongue, Jeriah," I ordered. Looking puzzled, Jeriah stuck out his tongue and held it with his grubby fingers. Yeah. I half expected that one. I turned to Albert. "If I could make it possible for you to brew this . . . uhm . . . drink, will you leave this place and move on peacefully?"

"What? Can you really do this, short shit?"

Pausing a moment, I reminded myself that I was paid to do this job, and I would not beat this ghost senseless with my staff. "I am an undead necromancer. I do believe I can arrange something. If I do this thing and you have your answer, will you leave The Purple Unicorn and move on?"

"Yes! Yes! I only need to know where my brew, Albert's Cosmic Kaleidoscope of Color, stands against Jeriah's!"

Give me the list of the ingredients you need, and my agent will set it up for you," I told him. With a snap of my fingers, I produced a pen and a piece of paper that he could use in his state.

"Really?" he exclaimed, as he grabbed my arms. A spark crackled as he made contact with my staff. I could have smiled, as he pulled away from me violently. Brushing down his clothes, he looked at me. "You aren't so bad for a midget." Beating him with my staff could be so satisfying.

"Enough of your comments on my height and lack of. Give me the list," I ordered, as I handed him the pen and paper.

He eagerly wrote down a list of things with very little pause for thought. Turning back, he handed the paper to me. Glancing over the words, I was impressed. It was not just a bunch of random scribbling. Alas, I had been around Kel too long, and I expected everyone to be like him. With a nod, I made my way to the door just as Tallon burst through. Before he could enter the tavern properly and flirt with Kelly (Thus, being rendered unconscious and useless), I took hold of his arm. Turning him around to face me, I handed him the list.

"You want to save the Purple Unicorn, yes?" I asked.

"Yes, but . . ."

"I have a job for you. Go get these supplies for this brew. Have the merchants put it on Jeriah's tab."

"Hey! Wait a minute! I ain't running no charity here!" Jeriah protested.

"If you want the job done, you will pay the price," I replied coolly.

"Bloody lich! Can't you just blast him into the beyond or something?"

Actually, I could if I wanted to do so, but it was so nice seeing Jeriah squirm. Despite being the monster that I profess to be, I have always felt that when dealing with ghosts, it was better to have proper closure. They were less likely to come back that way.

"You paid me to do this job, and this is how I do things," I answered.

Jeriah grumbled a curse at me that was technically true. (My parents were never married.) He turned to Tallon. "You'd best only get what's on that list, boy, or I will take it out of your hide!"

With a jump, Tallon stopped gawking at Kelly and threw Jeriah a salute. Without further delay, he left for his mission.

"I will put your spirit in a proper vessel to do your work," I informed Albert.

Moving across the room with the use of a levitation spell, I stopped at the table, where Bloodstone and Max were still playing their game. Max was on top the table again and scrutinizing the results of his latest throw. His butt was up in the air and his tail, curled in thought. Levitating myself up high enough, I grabbed hold of his tail and lifted him up. I held him at arm's length and took him over to the bar, where my clients were.

"Hey! I was about to win the biggest prize of them all!" Max yelped, as I dropped him on the floor. "Bloodstone's boots! I bet I could scrape a banquet out of those things that would be fit for a king!"

"It will have to wait. I have a job for you," I explained. Looking to Albert, I continued. "I need the use of your body. You will play host to this fine spirit here."

"No! No Way! Never! My spirit is enough for this body! Thank you very much!"

"And what can I do in a worm-eaten kobold body?" Albert complained.

"It's flea bitten, I will have you know! I ain't got the worms no more. That was last week's special," Max corrected.

"Shut up, the both of you!" I ordered. "Albert, you want to make this brew, and you need a set of physical hands of someone who knows his way around the kitchen."

"Grr . . ." grumbled the ghost.

"Max, you want to keep your job and your home, do you not? If the ghost is not appeased, then there will be no Purple Unicorn."

Max stood up straight with his fists on his hips. "Makes no never mind to me. I'd go live with Tallon at the tower."

My jaw tightened. Did these idiots have no place to go other than the tower? "I will have you stuffed before I allow that to happen!"

"Yeah. You ain't the master of the tower. Nikodemus is, and he likes me."

. . . And about everyone else he meets. Someday I would wrest that tower from his control, and I would incinerate all these fools and their town! Unfortunately, today was not the day. Nikodemus! He was the key to my dilemma! The load on my shoulders eased off. My jaw relaxed, and I almost laughed. Looking down upon the filthy dog, I wished that I could have shown him the wicked smile I felt.

"Fine. You can do that. Of course, Nikodemus will insist upon you taking baths. He's none too fond of stinky things residing at the tower. That's why Bloodstone does not live there. Even Kel takes regular baths."

All bravado drained out Max, as if I had cut an artery. "Really?" he asked. Swallowing hard, he looked to the ghost, then at me. "Alright. I'll do it, but I want my body back when you're done."

"Once I have my competition, I will be satisfied," Albert announced. "Even if I must be a rat dog to do it."

"That's kobold to you, sir!" . . . as if there was a difference.

Max climbed atop the chair next to Albert and glared eye to eye with him.

Gingerly, I took hold of Max's wrist. I had dealt with corpses with less vermin on them, and I really had no desire to have a share of his. Leaning my staff into my shoulder, I took hold of the ghost's wrist. Without giving either being a chance to argue further, I pulled Albert forward and threw him into Max's body. Yes. I could have done this in a more dignified way.

The spell took hold, and Max's mouth opened wide, and he fell backwards with the chair. Laying spread-eagle on the floor, he had one of those expressions like he had after sharing that peace pipe with Kel. I guess it was a cosmic experience. I had never infused my spirit with a living body. Although the living soul went to sleep for the duration of the possession, corpses were much easier to control.

After a few moments, Albert sat up in Max's body. He looked around himself with wonder, but the elation was soon quelled. A sour expression crossed his face. Puffing up his jaws, he spat and sputtered.

"Oh good gods! What did the little monster put in his mouth before I inhabited him? A cow turd?" Albert complained.

"Moo!" answered Taurus, as he dug around in his tunic. After some vigorous searching, he produced a jug of milk and handed it to him.

Albert gave a quick nod of thanks and downed it. He swished the liquid around in his mouth for some moments before he swallowed it. "Thank you, my good fellow. That's much better."

Once that was done, he walked around with his hands held out for balance. It did not take long for him to adjust to his new size and solidness. What a pity. It would have been more entertaining to see him run into chairs and tables and even smash into a wall.

"Let's do this!" he announced with more authority than Max ever asserted in his entire life. "To the kitchen!"

With his head held high, he marched to the backroom. Grumbling, Jeriah followed. With a shake of my head, I followed them. Despite my misgivings I had of the hell I was about to enter, I had to make sure that Albert did not seriously hurt Max's body. Nikodemus would not take it lightly, if I allowed the victim of my spell to die. Besides, Max had not done me any wrong.

The kitchen was a filthy sty like what one would come to expect from such an establishment. The ache ran throw my spine, as I looked around the place. I strained my senses for any sign of the type of vermin that came with hunched furry bodies and scaly tails. Finding none, I allowed my bones to relax back into place. After all, rats were a kobold's favorite food. Max had done his job well.

The walls of the room had been white tiles at one time. Now they were covered in a brown and black lichen. A fire roared in the fireplace. A seething cauldron with an unidentifiable substance floating in it, boiled over the sputtering fire. The stench would have choked me if I still drew breath. I should be the one creating such horrors, not these fools!

A huge still dominated the whole back wall of the room. Black bands, straps, and old pieces of cloth held together tubes and baubles. A dripping of a clear liquid pinged into a bucket at the end of it. The stench from this thing rivaled the cauldron. This was what I was here to save!

Nestled between these two smelly devices was an area with a filthy blanket. Multiple odds and ends were scattered around the area. Mostly, these things were broken tubes and the bones of small animals. A few kitchen utensils were in the piles as well. This had to be Max's bed and his treasure trove. No one else would want this stuff!

"How do you function in this place?" Albert complained.

"It's my kitchen and my still! No one else's and I'm proud of it!" Jeriah announced as he tugged at his apron. "If you don't like it, work somewhere else!"

"Fine. Back to the dining room," Albert insisted. "I will build my own still there, after all, I wrote down the needs for such on the list. I don't trust your trash."

"You'd do anything to ruin me!" grumbled Jeriah.

Speaking of Tallon and his errand, he came into the dining room with a hulking bag on his shoulder. Flexing his muscles, he strutted in front of Kelly. Never mind he was likely using a spell to lighten the load to nothing. Kelly was as impressed as one would expect. She pulled a mirror from her apron and began doing her hair.

Albert ran to the bag that Tallon deposited on the floor. He immediately crawled inside it like a cat. Rummaging around inside it, he threw out all the stuff on the floor. After several moments, he reemerged from it. Counting on his fingers, he took inventory of his stock. Without a word, he started to assemble his still.

During the hour it took him, I brought out a spell book from my storage dimension to study. Tallon did his flirting with Kelly and found himself unconscious. Bloodstone and Taurus picked up the Ships and Buckles game. Jeriah intently studied the work of the ghost. He probably never seen such intense work out of any of his employees.

With a final adjustment to the still, Albert nodded. He set about mixing the sugar, water, corn, and other things best not mentioned. Finally, he stood up proud. "All the ingredients are mixed and ready. Now all we have to do is wait a couple of weeks for it to ferment properly."

"What?" complained Jeriah. "I never had to wait that long for my stuff to ferment!"

"That's because your stuff is rotten to begin with," Albert pointed out.

"I am not waiting here for two or three weeks for your ingredients to simmer," I complained. I stepped between the two of them before Jeriah could grab hold of Albert and throttle Max's body. "I have better things to do with my time than stay at this disgusting tavern." I made my way to the concoction and looked down upon it.

"It can't be helped," Albert told us. "Do you seriously think that I like being in this mongrel's body?"

"You do have a point there," I remarked. "Then I will have to move the progress along. I have been a necromancer for near 600 years. I think I know something about rotting things."

Picking up my staff, I invoked the spell through it. I plunged it into the mixture. Within minutes, it fermented to a proper brown sludge.

"You're a natural at this!" Albert exclaimed.

"Indeed! Can I hire you on at the Unicorn?" Jeriah asked with wide eyes.

"No," I replied flatly. "I have to get Kel back into this hell hole. I am not about to move into his abode. Besides, you would not like to pay my price."

"You've got a point there," Jeriah muttered.

Rubbing his hands together, Albert danced around the still. "Now all I've got to do is distill it a couple of times. It should take a couple of hours, and it will be done. Prepare your taste buds for a delight they won't soon forget! Albert's Cosmic Kaleidoscope of Color is about to make its way!" Albert announced.

Shaking my head, I did not feel inclined to point out that I no longer had taste buds. I settled down again with my book.

6

It was time to wake Tallon from his beauty sleep. Standing over him, I had to admit that I liked him better this way. Best would be dead, but we cannot have everything. Of course, he was most definitely quieter this way. Alas, I had a job for him, and it was essential that he be awake for it. Being a wizard, I avoided physical labor and did most things with spells, but I found brute force would be the most satisfying approach to this situation. I gave him a firm kick. Despite my small size and fragile appearance, I could put quite a bit of power into this action. Tallon gave a grunt, but he stayed down. With a curse, I hit him across the back side with my staff. That method worked with excellent results.

Tallon jumped up with a high-pitched yelp. Turning around and holding his smoldering backside, he gave me a glare I wished I could reproduce on my own. Shaking my head, I remembered the trouble I had when I had flesh and blood. I was contented as I was.

"I have work for you, boy."

"I'm not your apprentice to order around," he answered, as he made his way back to Kelly with a swagger in his hips.

My fist clenched. I swore that I would never take on an apprentice! A spell that would boil the flesh from his bones came to mind. With an effort, I reminded myself that I needed this fool for this task. Running my fingers along the surface of my staff, I knew how this idiot's mind worked.

"It involves drinking," I told him.

"It does!" he exclaimed mid-stride. Turning around on his heels, he headed back to the bar. "You should have said so in the first place!"

"Bloodstone!" I called out to the filthy dwarf, who was still playing Ships and Buckles with Taurus and still losing. Granted Taurus was marginally smarter than Max.

"What do you want, Boneman?" Bloodstone answered.

"Come. Sit at the bar, the both of you."

Surprisingly, I did not receive more argument from either of them. Of course, I was saving Bloodstone from more humiliation, and booze was a great incentive for both of them.

"Kelly!" Jeriah called out. "Get your prissy tail over here and do your job!"

"I'm busy," she replied, as she inspected her reflection from different angles.

"Get over here now, you hell cat! What do I pay you for?"

"You don't pay me."

"If you don't serve these men, you aren't going to get a tip from them," he pointed out.

"Already got all their money."

"Wench!" he spat, as he made his way to the back room. He returned with two steaming mugs of his finest brew that he fondly called Dragon's Wrath. The liquid bubbled and boiled like the most potent poison known in this dimension. The scaly tail, hanging out of the mug, only added to the aura of the drink. When Jeriah threw the mugs on the counter, the liquid churned and made volatile rumbles. The gaseous emissions were enough to choke the average person. I was certain that given the chance, I could derive a potent, corrosive poison from this stuff.

Jeriah held out his hand for payment. "Pay up, you bums! You owe me for both drinks. I had to pay for the ingredients for Albert's brew, so you will have to pay for it as well."

Tallon and Bloodstone rifled through their clothes for their coin purses without success. This would have gone on for quite some time, since I was certain that Kelly had been quite thorough in her acquisition of tips.

"Put it on my tab," I told Jeriah.

"No," he protested. "Your food and drink tab is only for your consumption only."

Yeah, like I was going to use it. Even if I still had a stomach, I would rather starve and go thirsty than dine here.

"Fine. Put it on Nikodemus' tab." After all, Nikodemus was the one who invited Kel to stay at the tower. The whole reason I was in this cesspool was Nikodemus' fault. He could pay for a few drinks.

"Drink up, boys!" Jeriah proclaimed, as he took out a notebook and pen and scribbled down some numbers.

Albert bounced his way up to the bar with a mug in each hand. Looking up at the impossible distance, especially for one, who was now only three feet tall, he paused for a moment and blinked his eyes. In that instance, he did something that Max never did, he gave thought to his situation and how to resolve it. Placing the drinks on the chair next to the customers, he climbed onto the next empty chair. This brought him high enough to the bar. From here, he moved the mugs to the counter. Jumping onto the counter, he moved the mugs next to Jeriah's drinks. Once everything was situated, he dropped back down to the floor.

The lizard tails, hanging out of the Dragon's Wrath, stood up to attention. After a moment, they waggled menacingly at the new comer. Calmly, I moved between the drinkers and took hold of the tails. I flicked them each back into the proper mugs. I cast a protection spell over Albert's drink. I would have no interference in this contest. I wanted to return to the tower and delve into more forbidden lore and magicks before I and everything else around me turned to dust.

Tallon and Bloodstone each took up their mugs of Jeriah's famous brew and moved to clink them. They missed miserably, and they were sober at this time. Some of Bloodstone's drink splattered onto the chair next to Tallon. The chair collapsed into a pile of ash. Tallon's drink splattered onto the seat of Bloodstone's pants. Smoke curled up from the clothes. Covering my eye sockets, I hoped to avoid seeing a sight worse than the deepest abyss. Clenching my jaw, I, unfortunately, had a duty to perform, and I could not trust Jeriah to adhere to the laws of fair play. When I allowed the vision to return to me, I was relieved to see things were not so terrifying as I expected. The smoking hole in Bloodstone's pants only revealed white undergarments with pictures of little mugs on it. I was not sure how the paradox of clean, white undergarments on a filthy dwarf with filthy clothes worked, and I really did not want to know.

With all ceremonies done without casualties, I took hold of their nearest arms. "Do you have your sobriety remedies?" I enquired.

Rifling through his clothes, Tallon produced two vials of a swirling, dark liquid. "Never go drinking without it," he answered.

"Bloodstone?" I asked.

"What self-respecting dwarf would not carry such a remedy? Of course I have it!" he replied, as he slammed a flask on the bar. It looked like the same as the one with his dwarven brew, but it had a big red "X" through the mug.

Holding back the drinkers a moment more, I cast a spell to ascertain the alcohol was not tampered with. Nodding with satisfaction, I withdrew. "Drink up!" I proclaimed.

Each drinker hefted his mug of Dragon's Wrath and downed it with explosive results. Bloodstone's beard caught fire with a bright green flame. Tallon beat his chest and let fly a flame throwing belch of a similar color. Shifting his hips, he let fly a flame from his behind that ignited Bloodstones clothes.

Being used to such results from his clientele, Jeriah pulled out two buckets from under the bar. He doused each of them with cold water. Once all fires were drowned, Jeriah took out the pen and pad and wrote down more figures.

"That was your best yet, Jeriah!" Tallon exclaimed.

"Hic!" concurred Bloodstone.

Woozily, the two tried to grasp their sobriety formulae, but fell face forward before they could reach it. That was indeed a potent brew for Jeriah. Two out of the three previous times that I had been here, I saw these two down four of these Dragon's Wraths before passing out. Shaking my head, I pulled up Tallon's head by the hair and poured the sobriety potion down his throat. Hopping from the floor, to the chair, to the bar, Albert took up Bloodstone's flask and did the same for the dwarf. Jeriah stood back and puffed out his chest like a proud ground hog.

"Beat that, you spook!" he challenged.

"Yeah! Wait till they come back around, you fraud!" Albert spat.

Jeriah balled his fists. "I'll show you fraud, you has-been brewer!"

"Just try it, you shyster!" Albert replied, as he stood on the counter with his little fists up.

The ghostly audience gathered around and cheered, "Fight! Fight!" Several bets were placed. I am not sure what ghosts had to bet, but old habits die hard.

As much as I would have liked to have seen them bloody each other, I did owe it to Max to keep his body safe.

"Save it for the afterlife, you two, "I growled, as I separated them.

Meanwhile, the two contestants woke up. Climbing to their feet, they staggered around like zombies until the antidote made it into their systems proper. Having spent a good portion of their lives drunk, the both were experts with these potions. After a half an hour, Tallon and Bloodstone exited through the back door to relieve bladder issues. When they returned, they were ready to drink again. I cast a spell to make absolutely sure they were sober. With a nod, I had my confirmation.

Tallon and Bloodstone returned to the bar.

"Here it is. My masterpiece, Albert's Cosmic Kaleidoscope of Color," Albert told them.

Without hesitation, the two contestants took up Albert's drink. It was a clear liquid with a pale amber tint to it. Nothing was special about its appearance. After all, it did not seethe, hiss, or otherwise try to attack the drinker. Puzzled, Tallon and Bloodstone looked at each other.

Tallon pulled his mug up to his face and sniffed it. Pulling back, he frowned. "It smells sweet . . . like Aunt Maybe's pies."

Sniffing at it, Bloodstone nodded. "That it does, boy." He lifted the mug and saluted Tallon.

The liquid splashed onto the counter. When it made contact, there were no corrosive action nor fumes. Instead, the liquid just sunk into the wood, and a bright green moss formed. A pink daisy with a yellow center popped up. "Yee Hah!" it exclaimed, then a little red tongue stuck out of the center. Without hesitation, Jeriah smashed it with his palm.

"We'll have none of that! Kel is away now, and I want to enjoy the silence!" he griped.

The contestants shrugged at each other. Without more delay, they downed the drink in one gulp. It did not take long for it to take hold of them. They each sat upright with wide eyes. Sparkles and swirls filled their orbs and the utterances of "Ooo!" and "Aaah!" fell from their mouths along with unsavory saliva. Little stars and flower petals floated from all orifices and exploded with a sweet, intoxicating smell. Tallon and Bloodstone slid out of their seats like molten lava. Convulsions took them in the most fascinating dance I have ever seen. They stiffened and fell unconscious. Too bad. If their bodies had exploded, it would have been more entertaining for the audience.

Although I preferred them in this state, Albert and I had a duty to perform. With a determined resolve, we poured the sobriety potions down their throats. Again, after the proper wait, they opened their eyes and sat up dazed. Once their eyes were no longer glassy and they were as coherent as they were going to get, I felt it was time to be done with this daft contest.

"So?" I asked them.

Jeriah crossed his arms and glared at each of them in turn. Albert tried to stand up tall. That was impossible in Max's body. He gave up, and instead he twisted his hands and hopped foot to foot. Judgement was delivered upon him soon enough.

Scratching his head, Tallon looked from Jeriah to Albert and back again. "Jeriah, the Dragon's Wrath was fantastic as always, even better than usual, but that new stuff . . . .Albert's Cosmic Kaleidoscope of Color . . . Wow! That would put any dragon to shame. I would like to know how long it would keep me in that joy of drunkenness. I give it my vote."

"I have to agree with the knucklehead wizarding fool here. This brew would do Althgar proud. I feel that I could grow a whole new beard in places that no dwarf has ever grown a beard before! May you share your brew in the Afterlife with Althgar."

"Blagh! What do you two know! You're still under the influence of my Dragon's Wrath!" Jeriah growled.

Kelly walked by the still and drew a mug of Albert's brew. She sniffed it and frowned. She downed the mug with the vigor of the veteran drinkers. She stood in place for a few moments. Her face deep in concentration, then she nodded.

"This is some good stuff. It beats Jeriah's garbage no doubt," she remarked. Tossing the mug to Jeriah, she headed to the stairs and her quarters.

"Hey! Who asked you, Miss Puss?" Jeriah complained, as he looked down at the empty mug. With a growl, he threw it across the room. "You're a woman! What do you know of manly drinks?"

"Enough," she replied.

"That drink cost me! And it's going to cost you, missy!"

"Yeah, yeah. Take it out of my pay," she remarked, as she waved him off. She disappeared up the stairs.

"Grr!"

"Accept it," I told him. "Albert has won."

"I'd be willing to share my recipes with you, if you like. After all, I have no use for them anymore, and it is enough that my art lives on," Albert told him.

"Think of it, Jeriah," Tallon encouraged. "Mix your Dragon's Wrath with this stuff, and no one could beat it. It could be a Cosmic Dragon!"

Jeriah scratched his chin in thought. "You've got a point there."

"In the meantime, give us another round of both!" Bloodstone suggested. "After all, Nikodemus is paying, and no self-respecting dwarf would pass up free drinks!"

My job here was almost done. Unfortunately, I had to wait around for Jeriah to get all the recipes and brewing instructions from Albert. Meanwhile, Tallon and Bloodstone had another round of Albert's Amazing Alcohol (self-served) and ended up unconscious on the floor once again. Since they were no longer needed for anything, no one administered sobriety potions.

Taurus shook his head sadly, as he looked down upon Bloodstone. With a mournful moo, he picked up the dwarf by his ankles and threw him over his shoulder. With his load secure, he headed out of the tavern.

I looked down upon Talon. He could remain on the floor. It is true that I could take him back to the tower easily enough through spells, but he was safe enough on the floor here. In his absence, I might be able to get something done.

Once Jeriah was done doing his note taking, I pulled the ghost from Max's body. With eyes opened wide, Max hiccupped and fell face forward unconscious. Looking at the kobold's sprawled body, I could see the glow of his life force intact. No one moved to revive him. Of course, he would have had a major temper tantrum over not getting Bloodstone's boots. No one wanted to hear it.

Albert bowed to Jeriah. "Thank you, good brew master. Take good care of my recipes." Turning to me, he smiled and bowed. "And thank you good, ghost master."

"Get out and good riddance! It's a fortunate thing that you are already dead, or else I would have to kill you myself!" Jeriah rumbled.

With the movements of my left hand, I sent Albert and all the other ghosts back to where they belonged. Having succeeded in his task, Albert would move onward to the World of the Dead with no more problems. Such were the ways of ghosts.

"It is done," I told Jeriah.

"Good! Now, get out! I have work to do!" he answered, as he eagerly headed back to the kitchen.

Having already been paid, I had no reason to remain in this sludge pit. I wasted no time in getting back to the tower. I had work to do and an eviction notice to deliver.

7

Wasting no time, I returned to the tower and its massive library. In my free hand, I held a jar of the potent potion that Tallon had created by mixing Jeriah's Dragon's Wrath and Albert's Kaleidoscope of Colors. I was unsure what I would do with such a thing. Maybe I could pickle some species in it. The thought that this being Kel's final destination came to mind. At least he would not make so much noise in that state.

Kel was still there in the library when I returned. This, I expected. Strangely, he was quiet. This was the last thing I expected. He sat at a table and was furiously scribbling down in a brightly colored book. What a waste of ink and paper! Leaning my weight on my hands, I hovered over his crouched form. He did not acknowledge me or even look up. I did not really think he would. Of course, most beings did not notice me, and Kel was usually elsewhere mentally.

"You can go home now," I informed him. "The ghost is gone."

"Hey there, Grateful Dead Dude! When did you get here?" he exclaimed with a bright smile, as he looked up at me with glassy eyes. I remained silent. With a shrug, he returned to his work. "I don't wanna go. The acoustics in this place are fantastic! It is way out groovy, man, and the food ain't bad either. I've never sounded better! I've got to invite my band of wailing banshees here! They would sound stellar in a place like this!"

"What about your garden back at the Unicorn?"

"It can take care of itself. This place is every artists' dream!"

It was more like my own nightmare. Giving the problem thought and hefting the mixed drink in my hand, I thought about throwing it at him. Knowing my luck, it would ignite the place. I could give him the drink and hope it would knock him out, then I could toss him out a window. It would not work. Given the unusual substances he had ingested on a normal basis, I doubted anything could knock him out.

Shifting my jaw, I concentrated harder and I found the solution. "You know, Jeriah might send Max to an unattended garden, and he might make Frog Stroganoff with a leafy salad."

The colorful bard sat up straight and uttered some equally colorful words. "Oh no! Jeremiah would be mightily upset with me! My 'shrooms! Smokey would be most cross with me if I didn't have any 'shrooms to smoke with him! My weed! No way! I'm coming to rescue you, my buds!" he cried out. Grabbing his book, he made his hasty departure in a swirl of colors. That was easier than I thought!

Ah, silence at last! With that irritation gone, I made my way to my favorite section of the library. Looking over the titles, I chose one entitled *Ethereal Eviscerations*. Satisfied, I made my way back to my room. Settling down at my desk, I placed the jar of spirits down. I wasted no more time and immersed myself in the material before me and the graphic illustrations. Ah, I just needed some subjects to try this out on.

So deep was I in my studies, I did not notice Nikodemus' entrance until I sent a devastating blast in his direction. With that irritating, cheerful laugh, he not only dodged the blast, but he was able to contain it. Being a wizard, who cast spells just to find out what they would do, he was an expert at this technique. Sometimes I had to wonder how he had survived this long.

Turning to him, I crossed my arms. "You should not sneak up on the undead," I warned him.

"Why not? It's fun when you get ruffled!" he replied with that big grin.

"What do you want from me now?"

With an effort, he lugged a large rectangular box onto my desk and grimoires. Lucky for the both of us, the ink was dried. If it had not been, I would have to make a more powerful effort at blasting him to oblivion. Alas, lacking the power to do so was why I was in this predicament. Looking over this huge box, I noticed that the storage space would only be minuscule. Perhaps, if one trapped a soul in it, there would be confusing mazes and tunnels to torture the mind. I ran my fingers along its smooth surface. It was made of an element that I was not familiar with. Several knobs and levers adorned this box, and a solid netlike substance covered the hollows on either side of it. I wondered if these hollows could unleash some horrifying blast.

"And what is this?" I inquired.

"It is a great thing that I brought back from my travels. It mimics any sound that it hears."

With a swift movement, he turned some knobs and moved levers. A blast of the most terrible sound filled my room. It sounded very much like that horror known as Kel in the library, but the huge sound was trapped in my tiny room. I wanted to scream and find shelter. The noise was so disruptive that I could not cast a spell to destroy it.

Dancing around the room, Nikodemus announced over the din, "Kel made a recording of his concert in the library just for you, so you wouldn't miss him while he's gone."

Struggling, I grabbed the nearest thing- the jar of that disgusting, alcoholic, and potentially explosive potion and threw it. With a crash and a boom, the glass shattered on the device. Smoke and sparks rose from it, and the sound was no more. Coming up from my crouched position, I looked at Nikodemus.

"You destroyed it," he complained in a disappointed voice. With a shrug, he gave another big smile. "I will just have to get another one." With that, he took the remains of his vile device with him and left my room.

Looking at the shattered glass and wet floor, I knew that Tallon and I were even for that rot removing potion I had made for him now.

OF FAT RATS, MAD CATS, AND A COWARDLY COLLIE

By *L. N. Passmore*

In her weathered farm house for only two months, and already Elsie's list of pros and cons weighs heavy on the con side. Pro: back to nature, homage to Tinker Creek pilgrims she tells herself. Con: her two slightly crazed barn cats come and go through holes known only to them. Then there is the rat. And the suspicion the place is haunted.

"I'm a Romantic," she tells friends. "The view is to die for." Truth be told, its the cheap rent.

Someone had died in one of the upstairs bedrooms, but that doesn't stop her landlord from renting out his old home place. And yet . . . he can't seem to discard anything the deceased had touched. Furniture, stacked to the ceiling of the death chamber, blocks the door that cracks open a mere five inches. Most nights her cats racket about in there for hours, chasing mice—at least she hopes it's mice.

Each time storms rake her ridge top, the power goes off. So far it has come back on before she panics. This night, as the sun sinks below her hilltop road that winds into Slippery Ridge, West Virginia, the lights cut off good. And no storm for miles around to account for the power loss. A dusky October evening turns gloom-shot.

"Damn!" She calls to the cats, "Where did I put that flashlight?" No response from the absent menagerie.

She pulls a match pack from her jean's pocket and strikes a match, grateful that she hadn't given up smoking. Again. This week at least. Its gleam lights the way to the gas stove in the kitchen where she ignites the burner. In the warm glow she finds a flashlight in the junk drawer.

"Yes!" What a relief—the batteries work—so far great luck. But then she recalls where her landlord had pointed out the fuse box. In the cellar.

Except for the wind that whistles through loose siding and a looser roof, an eerie silence envelopes the house. The Ever-Sure's beam leads her down steps to a landing at the cellar door. As she opens it, her cats' screeches rise from the black depths. Something else rustles and bumps through the debris of the dank room.

Stay calm. She takes a deep breath, only to choke on a smell like dirty wet socks. *Ah, light switch! Flip the light switch.* Nothing happens. "Right," she says to the fusty murk. "New fuse, then light."

She points the flashlight directly to the wall opposite the door then down the thirteen rickety steps, the same oily brown as the wall. Past moldering paper bags and empty potato sacks, she makes her way, taking care not to knock over a rusted bucket filled with screws and bent nails. The first creak reminds her that the lower steps wobble. She stays to the left and leans against the foundation wall. Its rough-hewn logs and earth mortar snag her denim shirt.

Turning to the right Elsie plays her light on the far wall and locates the fuse box. Before her in the center of the cramped, wet space stands an oil furnace. It replaced a coal furnace, the reason for the now unused coal bin with its chute door to the outside. She breathes in the acrid odor of ancient coal dust and newly dripped oil. In best horror film tradition, she squiggles the light all around at the mouth to Hell where a freakishly fat rat nests among the chunks of old coal. She hears her cats in there growling at what must be the rat—so huge that even her collie Barney ran the night it had slunk through the unbolted cellar door. Her shriek and a tossed unabridged dictionary drove it back to its lair.

This time she growls, making her voice sound like a malfunctioning threshing machine.

Satisfied that Ratzilla won't attack, at least not before she gets to the fuse box, she sidles around the furnace to the wall with the fuse box and sagging wood shelves. The flashlight reveals dust-caked Mason jars crammed with what looks like some sort of biology class experiments floating in barnyard formaldehyde. Maybe peaches and green beans. All turned brown and fuzzy.

The shelf beside the fuse box holds a tiny paper container with new fuses.

"Thank God." Holding the light in her left hand, with her right she extracts a fuse and places it between her lips. The cold glass and metal feel good but taste bitter. She opens the fuse box door, wrangles out the burnt fuse, and pops in the new, praying it works.

"Topeka!" she screeches in her best George of the Jungle voice. "Light!"

The one naked light bulb, a dusty sixty watts screwed into a socket in a scarred crossbeam, reveals the true horror of the cellar.

Wet crawls up the grey, formerly white-washed walls. It slicks the rough-finished cement floor that edges into dull brown earth. Old wooden chests and paper boxes sit helter-skelter, their contents tumbling over the sides. Along the triangular wall beneath the steps hunch sacks of putrefying roots smelling of toe fungus. Their juices seep across the floor like tobacco spew. Almost anywhere she looks spider webs sag with long-dead flies.

The furnace crackles into life. She jumps, her heart pounding. Before she can catch her breath, the cats tear out of the coal bin, leap debris, and race up the steps. She dodges the old tin wash tub hanging from the beams and scurries after them around bags, ropes, and kerosene lanterns.

She shakes her head, marveling at the mystery of her landlord's life and all the crap he had abandoned. Upon reaching the top of the stairs, she flips the light switch, slams and locks the cellar door, then turns off the failing flashlight.

Barney stands there, waving his tail.

"Coward!" she scolds, but kneels down to hug him just the same. She makes a mental note to stuff a towel under the door . . . later, after a glass of wine . . . and a cigarette.

CLUTTER OR TREASURE

By *Alvena Stanfield*

Chris hurried to meet his golf buddies for breakfast at the club. With barely an hour until tee off, he double-timed it up the club's steps. Searching for his three pals he swayed side to side at the elegant dining room's columned entrance, Tony's waving arm signaled him to their table.

"We already ordered for you. Hope you wanted GC and waffles with bourbon maple syrup," Cameron said."

Chris nodded as he threw himself into the upholstered chair.

"Sorry I'm running late. My dog…"

"Is that what you're calling her today? Last night you called her--" Tony said.

"No, no, really. Duke is sick. I already phoned the vet. Left a message, asked for an appointment this afternoon," Chris said, sipping his grapefruit-and-champagne eye opener. He lifted his chin, squeezed his eyelids together, then slid his fingers across them.

"Hey, sorry man. You had that dog before we were in college, didn't you?"

"Yeah, he's pretty old. He puked up the whole condo last night. After we see the vet I'll order new carpet if--" Chris took a deep breath.

The three friends were relieved when the waitress set plates of food in front of them. Chris gulped the rest of his drink and sank his fork into his waffle. His cell rang.

"Help me Chris. They're stealing everything. Come quick," Grannie screamed.

Chris dialed 911, gave his grandmother's address and abandoned his golf buddies. Cruisers lined the street. Policemen clustered around the small woman seated on the porch. She was rocking, sobbing and twisting a brochure.

The "Yard Sale, Free Stuff" sign at the corner had clarified why she'd called. Women standing at the three tables marked "free," "cheap" and "make offer" stared at Chris as he raced past them.

"Make her go back home," Grannie said and stretched her skeletal hand toward him.

Looking down on the old woman Chris studied her pink scalp through straight white hair edged by an over-permed fringe. He took her hand then crouched down alongside her.

"Make who 'go back home,' Grannie?" She slung her arm in a half circle.

"Her, and them. She can't come here to visit, but today she can come, wrecking my life."

"I was afraid this might happen, Grannie. Over and over I asked you to come live with me and--"

"You got that big mean dog. He don't like me. He tried to knock me down last time I--"

"Duke's just like me, Grannie, big but harmless. You have to spend a little more time with him."

Recognizing Chris could handle this situation, the policemen nodded toward him, returned to their cruiser, then drove away.

"Your mother's here, that's who. The traitor. The back stabber. She put up those signs just as soon as she got here," Grannie whispered, then looked left and right, checking to see no one but Chris heard her. He stroked Grannie's hand.

"You know the neighbors complained to the city about the smell, Grannie. They served you papers more than a month ago, and the Health Department—"

"They got no right. It's my home." She tapped her thumb against her chest. "My home. She comes here and tells me she's 'made arrangements' and hands me this."

Grannie pressed the retirement home's brochure into Chris's palm. He smoothed it. Studying it, he smiled.

"Grannie, not only do they have beautiful rooms and daily road trips, they have happy hour from 2 till 4. I'll stop by for a glass of wine, maybe stay for dinner."

"You can do the same thing right here." She beat her small fist against the arm of her chair. "I'll get us a box of wine and--"

The creak of the screen door startled both of them. Chris's mother held an empty trash bag and a stack of newspapers.

"Oh, no, Emily, them's my memories. You can't throw away my treasures," Grannie said.

"Not treasures, just clutter and filth. That's what you've got inside there." Emily pointed toward Grannie's front door. Chris glared at her then at the newspapers.

"Mom, give them here. Grannie and I will sort through them. I can hire a Molly Maid for –"

"They won't take care of that mess. There's mice turds everywhere and, and, who knows what in that bathroom." She shoved the newspaper stack toward Chris then wiped her sweat-beaded forehead.

"It's a stinking pig sty. No wonder the neighbors complained. Just go look."

Chris ignored her and handed the top newspaper to his grandmother.

"Grannie, you keep the ones that are important and let someone else have the rest. My office staff will scan them or I'll have shelving built for them at the condo."

Looking over the rim of her glasses, Grannie studied the headlines. "See this here, Chris, May 12, 1981, above the headlines I wrote, Em and David birthed a boy 11:45 am. 7 lb 4. May name him Christopher after his grandfather or else Justin David." She clutched Chris's arm then leaned close so only he could hear.

"Your Grandpa was so proud of you. But you gotta hurry up and marry you a wife so's you can continue his name."

Chris smiled and nodded.

"This one stays with Grannie," Chris said.

His mother leaned forward, grabbed it from him and stuffed it into the trash bag.

"Nope. Green Meadows is all inclusive. Won't allow anything except her clothes."

Tears rolled down Grannie's cheeks as she pointed to the brochure she'd twisted so tight he had found it difficult to open. His mother stamped her foot, rattling the porch's unpainted wooden floor.

"I don't know what she did with your grandfather's money. She's broke. I checked her accounts. Now your father and I are on the hook. Three thousand a month. Well, we'll pay whatever Medicare doesn't," his mother said. Grannie sobbed and pressed a tissue against her eyes.

"Emily, you done turned against me."

Chris picked up another newspaper. Above its headline dated August 31, 1964 was scribbled. Cousin Charles, Ernie's boy, killed in Vietnam. He winced as his mother grabbed it and stuffed it into the bag.

"Go back home, Mom. Grannie and I will handle this."

Fists at her waist, glaring, she leaned close to him.

"I reschedule my work, pay for a thousand-mile flight, locate a pristine. I repeat, pristine, expensive retirement facility, convince them to make space for her and look at the thanks I get. You deserve one another. You, your stinking dog, and her---" She tossed the garbage bag toward Chris, grabbed her purse and stomped toward her car.

"You sure your dog won't run me over when I live there, so's I can take care of you?" Grannie said.

"I'm sure he'll love you like I do, Grannie, and you can come with me to the vet's this afternoon, ok?" Chris wrapped his arm around her bony shoulders.

"Page ten," Grannie whispered.

Shrugging, Chris found page ten, and a hundred-dollar bill taped to it. He raised his eyebrows.

Grannie smiled, then winked.

QUARTERLY REPORTS

By *Alvena Stanfield*

Fifteen minutes before quitting time Evelyn reviewed her time sheet and began entering its billing data into today's Excel sheet. She smelled her boss's Drakkar before he appeared.

"They've changed the quarterly meeting. I need those breakouts before nine tomorrow."

She leaned back in her chair and shook her head. "At quarter to five they, you, drop a bomb on me? Those reports take three hours," she said. Chin lowered, one eyebrow lifted, she stared at him over her eyeglasses' frames.

He smiled a big toothy grin but his eyes glared. He took a step closer.

"You're either a team player. Or you're not." Reaching into his pocket, he withdrew a pink slip and waved it toward her.

She felt her gut shrivel, imagining her children without toys Christmas morning. She gave him a weak smile and nodded. He pocketed the pink slip. Whistling, he strolled toward the elevator.

By 5:30 the sales-by-rep breakout was finished. Three more reports, twenty sets printed, collated, and stapled still remained. Knowing her children's daycare closed at six, maybe her mother could get them. She counted the rings: six, seven. Crossing her fingers, she hoped her mother's cocktail hour, hours, would begin later today. On the ninth ring she heard a clatter.

"Aw Shit," her mother said, hiccoughed, then "Hlo. Wo'sh thish?"

"Need to work till seven or eight," Evelyn said before she pictured her mother's driving when she was a kid, riding in a car that reeked of spilled beer. From the passenger seat Evelyn would give unwanted directions.

"Too far left, Mom," and "That was a stop sign."

"S-s-o you wanna me tget da kids…," her mother said.

"No, no, I'll get them," she said, deciding they'd be safer with her in an empty office building late at night.

When Evelyn reached the nearly empty third floor of the garage the automatic energy saver turned off overhead lights. The garage's outside lights cast alternating strips of light and shadows across the garage's floor.

Why did I park at the far end this morning?

She checked her purse and realized her keys had once again disappeared into empty gum wrappers and coupons. Half way to her car she hesitated near a dumpster and tossed in wrappers and coupons until her keys reappeared.

She heard the elevator doors click. Glancing around, and hating the company's energy conservation, she hoped she knew whoever had been on the elevator. But no one was there.

Maybe somebody hit the wrong button and got off on the second floor.

Twisting her keys between her fingers, pointed end out, she recalled the personal safety class she'd attended: jab keys in eyes or nose; kick genitals; scream "fire" not "help."

When she heard footsteps, she walked faster toward her car. As she hurried, nearly running, the footsteps got louder, closer.

Within a strip of shadow strong hands gripped her upper arms from behind and jerked her backward against his chest. She smelled cinnamon gum and felt his breath's warmth on her neck.

She screamed. Her scream echoed, but not for long.

WORKING FOR A CRIME BOSS

By *Alvena Stanfield*

The masked bank robber hit Della's shoulder with his fist.

"Shut them kids up or else," he said as he waved his rifle toward them.

Della stepped back and the robber pointed his pump action .22 at her.

"I'm just the chaperone."

The gunman lowered his chin and glared at the children's teacher. She screamed and passed out. Della took a deep breath.

"Sir, if I couldn't shut them up on the bus, I can't shut them up now. Let me take them out of here and back onto the bus," she said, trembling, as she pulled her son behind her.

"Right, so you can call the cops," the gunman said. Della shook her head.

"There's a good chance one of those tellers has already hit the silent alarm, let me get the kids out of your way." She looked toward the ceiling. "Those cameras see what you're doing. You'll look good to the police when they see you did the right thing and let the kids go."

Instead, the robber pressed the muzzle of his rifle against her ribs. She winced and let out a weak cry.

The second robber turned away from the counter where he held a large bag toward the teller. His shoulders lifted as he recognized his wife.

"Hey, she's making sense. Let her get them out of here. We'll be gone before the cops can…" he said.

"Daddy?" His son peeked around his mother. "We're playing a game?" he said.

Without breaking her gaze from the gunman Della swung her arm behind her and pushed her son out of the gunman's view.

"That's not your father," she said and glared at her masked husband. "Is it."

The robber shook his head and stared at the gunman.

"What the hell? Fix this, Man, or I'm killing them all." He waved his rifle in a semicircle. The teller screamed. The children pushed one another as they ran toward the exit.

"Hey, kids, we're playing a game. Get in a big circle on the floor," the gunman said.

As the children returned, joined hands and sat down, Della prevented her son from joining, keeping him behind her. The gunman aimed his rifle at the teller.

"Empty those cash drawers into the bag, and I mean this instant. Move or die," he said.

Nodding, her husband held the bag open as the teller tossed packs of banded bills into it.

"Please don't kill me. Please don't kill me," she said.

Della's husband glanced at his partner, then at his wife. He crossed the fifteen feet separating them.

"Let's go. Nobody's hurt. We got the money." He tried to hand the bag to the gunman.

"They know who you are, Man," He jerked the bag from Della's husband and fired into his chest. The teller and the children screamed. Sobbing, Della removed her husband's mask and knelt alongside him.

"Harold, don't die, please don't die, we need you," she sobbed.

"Daddy," her son said, watched his father lose consciousness. He pressed his fists against his eyes, rocking and sobbing.

The other kids rushed toward the exit, jamming it with their small bodies.

The gunman fired into the ceiling.

"Get away from that door." He fired again. Grabbing a small arm he slung the child onto the floor. Two more children landed alongside her as he tried to clear a path.

Outside the bank, a cruiser unloaded two policemen. A glance at the few screaming children running toward the school bus and at those jammed together in the doorway alerted the policemen many could die today.

"Police. It's only money. Don't make this worse. Don't hurt anybody," the older policeman yelled.

The gunman wrapped his arm under Della's son's armpits and swung him upward, using him for a shield. A few of the children screamed and scattered, trying to find a place to hide in the bank's lobby. Others pressed harder against those squeezed against the doorframe, unable to break away.

"Throw out your weapon," the older policeman shouted.

Instead, the gunman pushed his way into the crowded doorway. The terrified child-shield sent pee down the front of the gunman's slacks.

"You're the sniper. Do it." the older policeman whispered to the younger one.

He placed his .38 on his wrist, took a breath, held it and pulled the trigger.

Dropping his child-shield the gunman fell backward onto the children who were still trying to escape. Blood, bits of bone and brain scattered onto them from the baseball-sized hole blown through the back of the gunman's skull. The child he'd used as a shield sat up, staring without seeing, his mouth dropped open. No assurances by the policemen, Della or therapists could convince him of his safety, ever.

MEMOIR
AND
NONFICTION

IN JUST 1 YEAR, I EARNED $23,000 PUBLISHING MY FIRST BOOK!

By *Mikey Chlanda*

Eight surgeries down. Six more to go, and then a year or two of rehab. What was a fire lieutenant out on injury leave from being hit by a van and thrown 37 feet going to do?

Why, write a book, of course!

I needed something to take my mind off of the injuries and upcoming rehab. When I went to my college reunion that year, another former firefighter and I were talking to a guy that was on our college fire department 10 or 15 years before us. After he wandered off, Jeanne looked at me, and said, "Someone should write a history of Maples (the nickname for the department), before all these old guys die off."

"Hey," I thought, "I can do that!"

I jumped on it. I had the time, I had the knowledge, and most importantly, it would keep my mind occupied for the next year or so. I thought I would sell 50 copies. Maybe.

Fast forward a year. I sold 2600 copies and cleared $23,000! Holy crap, I think I can do this! Soon, I wrote a second, a record price guide. Then a third, soon followed by a fourth. I was hooked.

I did a lot of things right, most of them without even knowing what I was doing was right. I had some screw-ups, too.

Things I did right – first, I picked a subject I knew a lot about, and was passionate about. Ask any of my friends – when I meet someone, within two minutes they know I was a firefighter and now I write books.

The second thing I did right was crowdfunding that book on GoFundMe.com so I would have money to live on. Within five minutes of posting it one night, my old roommate from Antioch gave me $100. By morning, I had over $500. Anyone who gave me anything got a PDF of the book. For $25, they got a physical book, and for $100, they got a t-shirt as well, plus a deluxe hardbound edition. Interestingly enough, everyone else that gave me $100 or more besides my roommate was unknown to me. The sweetest one was from a woman that remembered I had saved her life back in 1989. (She went into anaphylactic shock from a bee sting and I gave her the epi shot.) This also gave me their email address, so I could tell them about my next book.

Antioch was also a huge help. They let me use hundreds of photos in exchange for donating five books to the library. For an out-of-pocket cost of $20, I saved a couple grand. That December, they published an interview with me. A few hundred books sold. Three months later, they published that interview in their print alumni magazine. A lot more sold. Then, they invited me to hawk my book at the reunion that year. The theme, amazingly enough, was authors who went to Antioch. Never underestimate how much your school will love (and promote!) you if you write a book about them. It only took me four years to figure this out – I've since done an Antioch coloring book, and am working on an early history book.

This one was total luck. I pitched Chris Brogan. He wrote back, "Holy cats. You can write. I'm impressed. Can I interview you? Please say yes." That interview went live the month before the book came out – I sold hundreds. Thanks, Chris.

Other things – I had a mailing list of former Maples firefighters to use for research and to sell my book to. Since the book involved local history, two local history groups bought a dozen books each. Being fire history, several fire museums bought – and continue to buy – books for their gift shop. You get the idea.

To date, I've sold over 4000 copies of that book, published 10 more, with 3 more due out this year. I make a full-time living writing books and articles, mainly fire-related. My work has been published by Huffington Post, Village Voice, Fire Engineering, Forbes.com, ESPN.com, and more. Good thing, too, as I never could again pass the physical again for the fire department.

A similar version of this story first appeared on Writer's Weekly, March 2017

DRUMMER JOKES

By *Mikey Chlanda*

The following jokes are excerpted from Mikey's *The Ultimate Drummer Joke Book*, available at amazon.com:

Q. What did the drummer get on his IQ test?
A. Drool.

Q. How can you tell that there's a drummer knocking on your door?
A. When you tell him to come in, he's two beats late.

Q. How many drummers does it take to screw in a light bulb?
A. 101. One to screw it in, the other hundred to say "That's not the way Neil Peart would have done it."

Alternate answer – None. Heck, they don't even realize it's dark in the room yet.

Q. What's the difference between a drummer and a homeless guy?
A. The homeless guy will eventually get his act together.

Q. What do you call a drummer's girlfriend?
A. A prostitute.

Q. What's the difference between a drummer and a puppy?
A. Eventually the puppy grows up and stops whining.

Q. What's the difference between a drummer and a government savings bond?
A. The savings bond eventually matures and makes money.

Q. Why are drummers always losing their watches?
A. Hey, if they could keep time, they wouldn't be drummers.

Q. What's the difference between a drummer and an extra-large pizza?
A. The pizza can feed a family of four.

Q. What does a drummer use for birth control?
A. His personality. And if that doesn't work, he uses the rhythm method.

FIREFIGHTING Q & A

By *Mikey Chlanda*

Mikey Chlanda is a most-viewed writer on various firefighting topics on Quora (a question-and-answer website where questions are asked, answered, edited and organized by its community of users.). He's working on another book, *Everything You Always Wanted to Ask A Firefighter, But Were Afraid To Ask.*, based on Quora questions. Here's a small sampling.

Q. What is the purpose for the Fire Department Connection on the outside of modern US buildings?

A. The FDC (Fire Department Connection) allows the engine to hook up and supply the sprinkler system to help extinguish the fire. Water pressure loses about 5 psi every floor, so if there's a fire on the 20th floor, there wouldn't be very much water coming out of the sprinklers at all after the initial building supply from interior tanks (or in older buildings, the large water tank you see on the roof) ran out. The water supplied by the municipality is generally around 50 psi when it comes into the building or out of the hydrant. An fire engine will take that same water supply and pump it out at 200 psi or more.

Firefighters can also access this water on the fire floor, so they won't have to make the stretch with hose from ground-level to the fire floor. Firefighters call it the high-rise pack - some bags containing couplings, hose, and a nozzle so they can hook up on the fire floor and fight the fire.

Q. Would firefighters in the same house ever be allowed to date or marry like on Chicago Fire?

A. Nope. It might be winked at on a smaller department, where there just aren't that many people to go around, but on my (smaller) department, nepotism is definitely frowned upon. Most/all large FD's have formal policies in place against this - as others have said, they would probably be allowed to work the same shift, but definitely not the same house nor the same rig.

Q. Is it safe to sleep with a candle lit?

A. Ummm….no. Why would you need a candle lit while you're asleep? Whatever possible reward you would get from it would be far outweighed by the (admittedly small) chance that it would start a fire, gutting the room, house, whatever, let alone potentially killing you.

I've been to several fires caused by candles igniting the curtains, pets knocking over the candle into flammable materials, etc. Just not worth it.

Q. Why do firehouses always keep Dalmatians as support?

A. This goes back to the days of horse-drawn fire engines. When an alarm would come in, the horses, who tend to be naturally skittish anyway, would start freaking out. Obviously this made it tough to get the rigging on them, let alone trying to get them to go to the fire. Some smart firefighter realized a) Dalmatians and horses seem to have a natural affinity for each other and b) Dalmatians, especially pure-breds, tend to be deaf. So the Dalmatians would just walk around the firehouse like nothing was happening, since they couldn't hear the bells and whistles. The horses would pick up on this and calm down.

Then the firefighters could rig up the horses and be on the way to put out the fire.

DAD IN THE MILITARY

By *Brad Hudepohl*

When World War II began, my father tried to enlist in the army, but the military rejected him because they discovered a heart murmur. He and my mother decided to get married, which they did in November 1942 at St. Monica church in Cincinnati's Clifton neighborhood. After my parents got married, the military decided to draft my father, and this time, they did not reject him.

Dad's basic training took place in Fort Collins, Colorado. While running the obstacle course, he managed to break both ankles and was sidelined several weeks. All of the men drafted with Dad were sent into the infantry. However, because of Dad's ankle injuries, he was not put into the infantry and therefore, was not sent to the front lines. If he had been, the history of our family might have been drastically different.

When his injuries were healed, Dad returned to finish basic training. One day the leader asked if anyone knew shorthand and typing. Dad raised his hand and wound up as secretary to General William H. Tunner in the U.S. Army Air Corps. His job was to type up reports, which included how many planes were lost or damaged the day before.

At that time, the U.S. was supplying the Chinese with equipment to fight the Japanese. The supplies were packed into C-47 cargo planes and flown over the Himalaya Mountains, also known as "The Hump". The Himalayas are the tallest mountains in the world. This was before there were pressurized cabins in the planes and the pilots had to wear oxygen masks. They wore leather jackets because of the frigid temperatures.

Dad was sent first to India and then to Burma. For security reasons, during the war it was not permitted to indicate in letters where one was stationed. My mother and father established a code system to pinpoint which country Dad was in at the time. Each closing to his letters, such as "With love" or "All my love", was coded to a particular country. This elaborate system gave my mother a little peace of mind, knowing where my father was.

Dad told me some interesting stories that happened to him during the war. Once, a pilot crashed a plane into another plane on the runway. The pilot, a lieutenant, was demoted to private. Dad took a few trips with General Tunner. On one trip they flew over French Indonesia, now called Vietnam. Another time they flew down the coast of India to Ceylon, now called Sri Lanka. The nose of the B-17 plane was made almost entirely out of glass. Dad told me that the view was breathtaking.

The most dangerous thing that happened to Dad occurred when he was stationed in Burma. Dad slept in a tent on an army cot and was a very sound sleeper. One night his tent caught fire with him in it. The other men in the tent carried his cot outside, with him still fast asleep. Dad didn't wake up until the next morning and was surprised to find his tent burnt to the ground.

During his time in India, Dad observed Indian culture. He visited the Taj Mahal in Agra and photographed it. The Taj Mahal was built in the seventeenth century by Mughal Emperor Shah Jahan to house the tomb of his favorite wife. The Taj Mahal is considered to be one of the most beautiful buildings in the world. Dad took other photographs of Indian life, such as one of an Indian snake charmer playing a flute in front of a basket with a cobra coming out of it. One thing Dad discovered he disliked during his time in India was the way the British colonizers poorly treated their Indian subjects. At the time it was common for Indians to work on British tea plantations for seventeen cents per week. They labored six days a week from dawn till dusk and were paid on their day off. The owners then forced the workers to wait in line all day for their pay.

Dad made it back safely from the war and even received a letter of recommendation from General Tunner for employment which I now possess.

MOONLIGHT MADNESS

By *Brad Hudepohl*

One night around 2 AM, my first wife Brenda and I were in bed sleeping when we were awoken by loud footsteps of someone running down the stairs of our house to the first floor. We heard the front door open, then slam shut. Then we immediately heard the door open and shut again. Someone ran back up the stairs and then down again.

Startled and shocked, my wife and I feared an intruder was in our home.

Not knowing what or who I would find, I got up to investigate. I went downstairs and looked out the front window, only to discover my son Jeff sitting patiently at the curb in the moonlight. He had his coat on and his book bag; he appeared perfectly prepared to go to school.

I opened the front door and asked, "Why on earth are you sitting on the curb at two o'clock in the morning?"

He said, "I'm waiting for the school bus."

You see, he thought it was 7 AM when he usually caught the bus, and that he was late.

"Son, come back in the house." I joked gently with him about his mistaking 2 AM for 7 AM, and we all went back to bed. It seems the moonlight causes many of us to do strange things.

I AM A PRINCESS

By *Elle Mott*

1967

The month of May often brings an end to spring rains, welcoming birds to the flowers sprouting for life. In 1967 racial upheaval ran the downtown streets of Little Rock, Arkansas. Birds and flowers likely went unnoticed in this turmoil. Challenging this upheaval, peace activists stood in protest against the Vietnam War.

Unlike the fight between love and hate, love blossomed when Elvis Presley married Priscilla Beaulieu in early May. Priscilla was a military daughter, young and charismatic. It was a princess-like dream envied by teenage girls in middle-class America.

Mother's Day was celebrated in mid-May, likewise as it had been for a half-century or more. Enacted by U.S. Congress, Mother's Day was an idea brought forward by Anna Jarvis in memory of her mother, Ann Reeves Jarvis, who had been a peace activist caring for wounded soldiers on both sides of the American Civil War. On Mother's Day in 1967 in Little Rock, I was born. More importantly, if only to my maternal side, I was born into a special place of our family lineage.

Toward the end of May, on the 27th, nine-year-old Caroline Kennedy christened the Navy's newest aircraft carrier, the "USS John F. Kennedy", after her father and our past U.S. President. My father, whose family roots were in Little Rock, was also in the Navy, stationed at San Francisco, California. Then, my mother took me 2,500 miles from Arkansas, denying me any childhood relationship with my father. Instead, I was destined to meet our family matriarch. With a high arch to her painted eyebrows and a magniloquent rhythm to her voice, Nana introduced me to relatives, friends, and strangers, "This is my first great-grandchild."

1977

Double-wide grand doors were ahead, blocked from our view by the growing crowd. An illuminated awning lit the sidewalk, and above that, a golden red sign flashed the title of its feature film. It was opening night for this Sci-fi in Portland, Oregon, an hour north of Salem where we were from. Back then, if you wanted to see a big movie, you'd get to the theater or else wait for years hoping it comes out on TV.

I remember it was the middle of the week because I wasn't allowed out after dark on a school night, but this was an exception.

Not because it was a big movie, but because I was with Cheryl and her dad, who was a well-respected man in our community. People mingled in line with us, some in costumes, but of characters I didn't recognize. They certainly weren't Pinocchio or Cinderella. Walt Disney movies on Saturday afternoons at the theater in downtown Salem were all I ever saw. A little girl in line next to us, even littler than me since I turned ten-years-old earlier that month, asked if we were with our dad. Not to spare a second in my reply, I said, "He's her dad. I'm best friends with the mayor's daughter."

Cheryl soft punched my arm. She was never okay with the attention from my gloating, but I couldn't help it. I was proud that Nana was proud I had chosen well in my friends. Who I played with was subject to Nana's scrutiny, needing her approval, if not outright picked by her. As her first born great-grandchild, I was expected to do no wrong. It was a tall order and usually, I could comply. When I messed up, though, it meant a lengthy lecture. Otherwise, my life in Salem was princess-like, far from the problem place where I was born.

In 1977, I held no memories of my birthplace, and instead only knew the bedroom community I was growing up in. Sloping green lawns edged by camellia trees, rose bushes, and noble firs bordered small estates of the Laurel Springs neighborhood. Important men and their families lived in this well-lined ranch-house sprawl. Tucked safely in our dens, the average family had a fireplace or two, the latest console color TV, and a crafts table. It was the place for us girls to get together after school for our Blue Birds or Camp Fire Girls meetings.

Girls' bedrooms were adorned with canopy beds in soft pastels, collectible dolls on display, Barbie dolls to play with, and a record player to listen to Captain and Tennille, Diana Ross, or my favorite, The Bee Gees. Bookshelves in our bedrooms held the Nancy Drew series and the latest in the Little House on the Prairie series. Dresser drawers held our plaid bell bottoms and blue jeans with flower patches. And in the closets, hung our many dresses.

Cheryl's dad put his big hands on our shoulders, with one hand on Cheryl, and one on me. He walked us into the theater as our turn in the line moved forward. Squirming in my seat next to Cheryl, I rooted for Princess Leia, who had to safeguard plans, which if fallen into the wrong hands, would destroy an entire planet. Would I ever do anything as important as Princess Leia? Would I forever make Nana proud of me?

1987

I navigated jagged edges among boulders for a smooth spot to sit. Natural rock in sun-drenched oranges and reds formed an arch as if pointing upward to the gods in the sky. At a much higher elevation than Northwest Oregon, Colorado's thick blanket of sunshine loomed above. It had been ten years since my evening with Cheryl and her dad; ten years since my princess dreaming had begun.

Under the rays of the Rocky Mountain skies, I was lulled into a spell of spiritual awe from the Garden of the Gods Park. On that day, as I turned twenty years old in 1987, I had only a new start in front of me. This new start could lead to something great. For a while, Portland life back in Oregon had been good. But, friends and I drifted different directions, and my temporary job at the Social Security Office ended. I should have been college-bound, married, and involved with something worthwhile, or so Nana would have wanted. Instead, I had been aloof, thinking I had time to figure my life out. Then, Nana had died before I could.

If only to appease Nana's powerful influence, I had to find my place in this big country. That's when I followed a girlfriend out to Colorado for her job offer. Where Portland quit working for me, maybe, just maybe, Colorado Springs was the place I could become the successful woman Nana had wanted of me. Only then, could I become the princess, as once hoped for by our family matriarch.

1997

On a lark, I was living smack-dab in the middle of our big country, and its stench of humidity stifled me. I wasn't yet convinced I belonged under hot rains and tornado watches. It was my third summer in Springfield, Missouri, and ten years later than my twentieth birthday in Colorado. It was a Monday and a holiday, Labor Day, which meant I had the day off from my desk job.

I pushed the up-arrows on the TV remote to hear the volume better. It was either that or else turn the window fan off. Every local TV channel had new stories of Princess Diana of Wales. I admired her because she had been a well-loved teacher, and then like a fairy tale dream come true, a royal princess. True to herself, she had stayed focused and determined in her social concerns. Well-revered, she was well loved worldwide.

On that Labor Day in 1997, the news left me astonished as if in disbelief. London's Princess had died. TV images of Princess Diana flashed with great frequency, intermixed with news coverage. Acres of white and pink flower bouquets donned the palace courtyard. She died when only thirty-six, and also born in the 1960s, same as me, but six years earlier. She married into her royalty, picked by the prince. Whereas, my long-lost claim to family legacy came from my birth. Diana had done well by making our world a better place, but I had fallen short by neglecting my honor as a first-born grandchild.

Ten-and-a-half years had passed since Nana died, but her voice still knocked at my thoughts. If only to appease my own self-made discord, Princess Diana's legacy instilled urgency for me to change. Determined to rectify my messes, I had to discover my place of belonging, whether in Missouri or somewhere else. My choices from then on out had to align with Nana's core values or else I'd be forever lost and without purpose.

2007

It was an especially warm season for southern New Mexico as I hurried to my next class. A shortcut led across the flat grassy courtyard, but like other students I favored the sidewalk shaded by our classroom buildings. It wasn't that the grass had been freshly manicured, but that grass didn't really grow in the sandy desert.

Once curious about desert living, its mesas soon became a familiar sight. In May, its surrounding mountain peaks popped oranges and reds, like fire opals and rubies on a princess's tiara. Although we never got snow in the cacti-lined desert, not even in December or January, the Organ Mountains were a four-season beauty. While Las Cruces was near-void of greenery and trees, its backdrop view made up for it. Yet, even at a towering 11,000-feet-high, they could only pretend to shade our sunbaked city.

The beating sun hovered over ninety degrees on that day of my fortieth birthday. That first full year of college pulled me up in math competency to be ready for college-level algebra. I liked math but found computers challenging. In my first semester, I had learned how to use a mouse and what email is. Nana would have liked our emerging information technology age, same as she had liked color TV, her car cell phone, and freedom to wear pantsuits instead of lady-dresses. She'd also have liked me in college before my fortieth birthday, rather than deep in wanderlust. Nana was long gone, but still, I persevered with my goal for a college degree, something she'd have been proud of.

That year, 2007, was a good year to run with my hope, or so that's the message I got from the positive vibes in our country. Earlier that year, Hilary Clinton announced her place in vying for presidency. Of course, it wasn't official for another seven months, in January 2008. Two biographies on Hilary would be out in the next month, June.

I recalled Hilary's autobiography published a few years earlier, in which she shared that while she is many great things, from mother to lawyer to the President's wife, she wasn't born any of those things. Rather, she worked hard to become someone. I too was working toward my goals. Determined to define myself, and to discover my purpose, I believed I'd soon make peace with Nana's wishes which permeated my daily decisions.

2017

I'm wearing a princess tiara. It's not a real tiara, but one of those plastic ones from the store where no matter what you buy, it's only a dollar. No real rubies on this crown, but still, I am as happy as a princess on this day as I emerge into the second half-century of my life. It's not life around me that makes me happy. Rather, it's who I am which reveals my happiness.

Actually, all isn't that great in our country now, or at least, could be better. Hilary Clinton never made it to the White House, or at least, not as President. The current presidential power leaves me disillusioned. If anything squelches my anger, it's my fellow women in my country who are speaking up, yelling out loud, and marching forward. Five months before, in January 2017, international marches for human rights and equality numbered in the hundreds with millions marching in protests. On our Capitol's front steps this protest was the largest political demonstration since the days of the Vietnam War, as was happening on the downtown streets the day I was born.

If only for a couple hours of a distraction from our worldly turmoil, my good friend, Janet and my bosom friend, Kimberly ensure I have a birthday party. It's a princess-like celebration to turn fifty-years old. My friend, Alvena is with us. As sweet as her never ending smile, she helped me find my house. A gift afforded from my late father's estate, it is the only house I've ever purchased. No longer traversing our country in wanderlust, I've finally found where I belong.

My dear friend, Lorene is with us at my party. She's been by my side since shortly after I arrived here, four years earlier in May. Wise, smart, and true to herself, living life with utmost honesty is how I'd describe Lorene; a trait I admire. She has helped me understand my life is not about living up to my family legacy. Instead, my life is about becoming who I was meant to be, and not who as a child, I agreed to become.

It's my commitment to my job at the Public Library in Cincinnati, my passion for writing, my community involvement, enrichening friendships, and the love for my pet finches, as well as owning my values that define my happiness. I remember Nana's love, not in what she expected for me, but for the courage, resilience, and fortitude she instilled in me. I feel my father's love, not with any memories to be had, but with heartfelt gratitude. And I wear my princess tiara, because I am a princess, if only because I'm embraced by love and hugs of my kindred friends.

A LITTLE BIT O' SOUL

By *Gary Reed*

There were no telltale signs that something memorable was about to happen. Just the opposite, in fact. It was the last hour of a two-semester, mandatory philosophy course. The professor, an ancient Jesuit priest, was lecturing in a low monotone. He was not making eye contact with us. He appeared to be focused on the point in the back of classroom where the ceiling met the wall, but was probably just staring into space. In short, if such a thing were possible, he seemed even more bored than we were.

This was a long time ago in a midwestern Catholic university. Back then, at least in that academic waystation, professors did not ask questions on exams about material they had not covered in class. With that in mind, some enterprising fellow students were blitzing the elderly priest with questions that had nothing to do with the subject of the day's lecture. It was an obvious ploy to reduce the amount of material he could cover, and thus, the amount they would need to study for the final exam.

This priest had two Ph.D.'s – one in philosophy and the other in physics. Plus, he had been a college professor for a *very* long time. There was zero chance he did not understand the game afoot.

Even so, on another day, I might have joined in the effort, if only to relieve the boredom. But that day, I was unusually relaxed. It was Spring, it was the last day of the academic year, and life was good. I just sat there, somewhere between philosophic and catatonic, waiting for the class to end.

But my classmates knew something that I didn't: This ancient cleric was one of the earliest activists in what would become the Pro-Life movement. When not teaching, he gave talks and busied himself sounding the alarm about the evil inherent in allowing women to control their own bodies. This was in the late 1960s, a few years before *Roe v. Wade*.

Redoubling their efforts, my classmates began throwing questions at the priest about abortion and birth control – not because they were interested in his views, but because those topics interested *him*. They evidently hoped the priest would not be able to resist the temptation of discussing something he actually cared about.

With that, the game took an interesting turn. The priest had a pained expression on his face. He knew full well what they were up to, but apparently, something about their questions betrayed a fundamental misunderstanding of the Catholic Church's position on abortion or contraception – a misconception he felt compelled to terminate.

"How many of you have heard an explanation," he asked the class, "of the Church's position on abortion and birth control?"

Only about one-in-four raised their hands. That in itself was remarkable, because most of us were completing our fourteenth or fifteenth year of Catholic education. We knew *what* the Church's position was, of course, but curiously, no one had bothered to explain it.

The old man acknowledged the show of hands, gave up on the assigned material, and launched into an abridged explanation of the Church's view.

He probably said a bit more than I remember, but essentially, he went to the blackboard and drew an "x" or some other abstract symbol to represent a sperm and a different symbol to represent an egg. He then drew arrows from each to a circle. The circle represented the ovum that forms when the sperm fertilizes the egg.

At the moment the sperm and egg unite and form a new cell, he explained, God infuses an immortal soul and transforms that cell into a human being – a person. Anyone who intentionally destroys that cell, or the embryo it develops into, kills that person. This wasn't about killing a cell or a bundle of cells; it was about killing a living being *with an immortal soul.*

I was probably nineteen-years-old then, and despite all the jokes about teenagers knowing everything, I was up in air about, *well,* pretty much everything. So, *how,* I wondered, did this priest *know,* with such absolute certainty, that God *infused a soul* into that cell, and did so at that *exact* moment?

Souls, so far I knew, didn't weigh anything, didn't have an electrical charge or cause a chemical change, and were not otherwise detectable. The Bible, obviously, didn't say anything about sperm DNA and egg DNA meeting and hooking up.

So, how did this frail old man *know* that God infused a soul, whatever a soul was, and did so at that precise moment, with such complete certainty?

Of course, I could not very well ask the old priest that question. I would have gotten a lecture about faith and the need to trust God, or something else equally uninformative. And quite possibly a lower grade. "Bad attitude" or "poor class participation."

But it occurred to me that there was something I *could* ask. Before my internal editor had a chance to head things off, my hand went up. I was sitting right in front of the old priest, and he nodded at me.

"If I understand the biology right," I said, "in the case of identical twins, that first cell, the zygote, splits into two new cells that separate and develop independently."

The old priest may or may not have nodded to indicate that he understood what I was saying. I don't remember. But he didn't cut me off.

"When that happens then?" I asked. "Does the soul that God just infused split in two, in some sort of spiritual mitosis, or does God recall it and issue two new ones?"

I think my question caught the old priest off guard, or maybe he was just distracted, because he muttered something about "divine foresight" and then lit into two guys sitting near the door. They had been having a whispered conversation between themselves for several minutes, and their conversation had become louder and more annoying.

Before the priest had gotten very far with those miscreants and could turn his attention back to me, the bell rang. He surrendered and dismissed the class, and I made my escape unscathed. The ancient professor had not eviscerated me, and God hadn't struck me with a thunderbolt.

But I left with lots of unanswered questions.

By "divine foresight," the priest meant that God knew what would happen in the future. God would, therefore, know in advance that my hypothetical zygote would split, and that the new cells would go their separate ways. So, God would wait until after they separated before going about the business of infusing a soul – or in this case, two souls.

In the late 1960s, a rock band called The Music Explosion had a hit song called "A Little Bit O' Soul." It was a catchy little tune. Once you heard it, you had trouble getting the damn thing out of your head. One couplet claimed, when "You're broke in two, You need a little bit o' soul to see you through."

Is that how it was with zygotes?

The obvious next question was not, "Well, what if the new cell splits again – as in the case of triplets or quads?" The answer to that was obvious – more Divine Foresight. God is all powerful and does *not* have a problem with premature infusion.

No, my next question would have been, "Sometimes the zygote simply doesn't attach to the uterine wall. It quickly dies, and the body discards it. Given Divine Foresight and all that, does God infuse an immortal soul into that poor, doomed cell anyway? Wouldn't that be a waste of a perfectly good soul?"

More to the point, wouldn't it be a cruel joke to tell that poor doomed cell it has an immortal soul and Free Will; to tell it to choose wisely or end up in Hell; and then, in the next second, say, "Sorry, time's up. Off to the After Life with you!"

If the answer to that question is, "No soul for you!" then that what happens if you stretch the time frame just a little? What happens when God knows that the embryo – or whatever the correct biological term is – will not spontaneously come undone immediately, but will do so a few seconds or minutes after forming? Does He inject a soul into the zygote anyway? Or given Divine Foresight, does God once again elect not to do such a cruel and useless thing?

If not, then what if the terminating event, spontaneous or not, doesn't occur for a couple weeks or months? Does Divine Foresight still come into play?

And whatever the answer, how do you *know* that with such certainty?

Father, forgive me, but at what point in human evolution did God begin this business of infusing souls? Researchers believe that hominids split from chimpanzees about seven million years ago. Scientists think that one of our forebears, a *Homo ergaster*, first domesticated fire about 1.5 million years go. Did the clever chap who first stared into a campfire have a soul? Was it a regulation human soul, or a different, less evolved model?

Archaic humans probably developed brains roughly comparable in size to those of modern humans about 600,00 years ago. The line that became *Homo sapiens* split from the Neanderthals roughly 500,00 years ago. So, what about Neanderthals? Did they have souls? And if so, did their souls differ from the souls of *sapiens*?

Scientists recently identified archaic *Homo sapiens* remains from about 315,000 years ago. The earliest modern *Homo sapiens* date to about 195,000 years ago. Scientists also believe that *Homo sapiens* underwent a remarkable "cognitive revolution" spanning about 75,000 t0 35,000 years ago.

This revolution did not significantly change the size of the brain, but likely involved changes within the brain. From about 35,000 years ago, *Homo sapiens* were not only recognizably modern humans, but probably had about the same level of raw intelligence.

Given this history, at what point did God begin this business of infusing souls into *Homo sapiens*? And how do you *know* that?

There are billions of galaxies, each with a billion or more stars, and vast numbers of those stars have planets. Many of *those* planets are, or were, or someday will be like our own. It is likely, scientists tell us, that there are, or were, or someday will be, sentient beings on at least some – and quite possibly, many – of those planets.

Does God infuse souls into little green men?

If you're raised Catholic, you learn early on that God is all knowing and all wise – way better at knowing everything about you than even Santa Claus. But back then, when as a young child I studied my Catechism, there were already over two billion humans on the planet. Today, there are three times as many, maybe more.

That's a lot of sperm and eggs and zygotes for God to keep track of. Does God ever get distracted, or peeved, and not infuse a soul into some zygote? Is that what happened to Hitler? And while we're on the topic of Hitler, what happened to Divine Foresight when that bastard was conceived? Why didn't the Almighty give that malevolent little zygote a gentle nudge off the uterine wall before things got out of hand?

My ultimate questions today are still the same initial questions that popped into my head back in that classroom in Alter Hall:

First, "How, kind sir, do you *know* that God chooses to spend His time infusing souls into zygotes, so that He can have the pleasure of rewarding some and torturing the rest for all eternity?"

And second, "Will this be on the *Final* Exam?"

I DON'T THINK THEY GIVE MERIT BADGES FOR THIS

By *Gary Reed*

In the early 1960s, if you were a top student and were interested in science, in your daydreams you might imagine one day becoming a nuclear physicist and joining the hunt for new subatomic particles. Or, you might dream of becoming an astrophysicist and mapping the cosmos. In real life, if you were that student, you got beat up a lot.

When I moved from grade school to high school, I graduated from the science fiction adventures of Tom Swift to young adult books about the physicists of the late 19th and early 20th century. Those were the men and women who gave us Relativity, Quantum Mechanics, the Big Bang, and the Expanding Universe. Their discoveries unraveled the "secrets" of the atom and the universe and gave us radio, television, radar, radio telescopes, the atomic bomb and the space program. It was heady stuff.

To be clear, I did not, ever, imagine that one day I might one day be among those giants, but I did imagine that if I could do well enough in math, someday I might be one of the many bright young men going into physics or a related field.

But if you were someone like me, you never, ever, talked about any that. Still, somehow, people could tell. You knew this, because one minute, your head would be in the stars, and the next it would be shoved inside your locker.

As a result, you couldn't help but notice the ads in the back of magazines that promised to transform you from a ninety-pound weakling to someone the bullies didn't pick on. But you had to be gullible not to know that those were scams. Still, if you were twelve or thirteen and you happened on a book about judo in your local library, you might be tempted to wonder what it would be like to be able to defend yourself.

And if you had a particularly strong fantasy life, or a death wish, one day on a whim you might check that book out and carefully study the pictures and diagrams describing various moves. Of course, no one learns judo (or later karate, etc.) from a book. It requires an instructor, lots of practice, and body strength. It also requires self-confidence. If you're smart enough to want to be a physicist when you grow up, you're smart enough to understand that and to return the book by its due date.

In my freshman year in high school, in addition to my school work, I worked at a local grocery store one evening during the week and on Saturdays. One evening after finishing work at the grocery, I left to walk home. It was just after 9:00 p.m. I could have taken a different route, but I chose the route that took me past the parochial high school I attended.

As I passed the school, a Boy Scout meeting ended, and ten or twelve boys, mostly eighth graders emerged. Somebody said something, and suddenly, the group came running toward me. They were going to beat me up, or at least shove me around, knock me down, and humiliate me.

I could have run, but didn't. As a high school freshman, I probably didn't want the humiliation of running away from a group of eighth graders and having them laugh at me – which is probably what they expected would happen. I continued walking at the same pace until the group surrounded me and prevented me from continuing.

At that point, I attempted something that would later become my favorite tactic for defusing tense situations – humor. I looked around at the group surrounding me and said, "Guys, I don't think they give merit badges for this."

The line got an appreciative chuckle. The group didn't seem to have a clear plan and appeared uncertain what to do next. Unfortunately, I knew what would happen. Someone would shove me, and then someone else would, and things would go rapidly downhill from there.

"What they do give," I said, "is suspensions. The minute the first *one* of you touches me, we all know what's going to happen. You will *all* be suspended from Scouts. Your whole unit will be disbanded. Everybody in town will hear about that, and they'll shake their heads, and ask: *What kind of screw up gets thrown out of Scouts?* Your parents are going to ask you the same thing: *What kind of screw up gets kicked out of Scouts?*"

I was probably more amazed than they were that all of that came out in a calm, more-or-less matter-of-fact tone of voice, but I believe I know where that bravado came from. I had just spent the summer before in Fort Lauderdale with my aunt and cousin. We spent every day at the beach, and my cousin and I spent most of our beach time swimming. By the end of the summer, I was in the best physical shape of my life, and after two or three months away from home, I was more self-confident than I'd ever been – low bars on both counts.

Unfortunately, group dynamics being what they are, none of my tormentors wanted to be the first to turn away.

"If more than *one* of you push or shove me," I said, "then all of you will probably be suspended from school too. Frankly, guys, beating me up isn't that big of a thrill. Ask anybody."

Unfortunately, logic isn't nearly as persuasive with a bunch of adolescent males as the fear of being seen as weak or not being part of the group. My little speech hadn't gotten me very far. The best I could hope for was that I'd planted the idea that this might not end well.

My father grew up in a tough neighborhood during the Depression and had been in lots of fights. He had often told me, or said in my presence, that when confronted by a group, pick out one guy – a leader, if you can – and make it between you and him. That was the rule. I had seen that play out lots of times in the movies and on television.

I recognized one of the guys in my group of tormentors. He was the cousin of one of my closest friends. He was also a genuinely decent guy. Plus, he had the strength of character and the smarts to be a leader. I decided I needed to make this between me and him.

"Bob," I said. "You're too smart to be a part of this. Your cousin is my best friend. What are you going to say to him when he finds out you were part of this? I've been in his home and met his mom and dad – your aunt and uncle. What are you going to say to *them* when they ask why you didn't have enough sense to walk away from this?"

He snorted derisively or made some other gesture to let his companions know he wasn't impressed.

"What are you going to tell *your* parents when they ask you how you could be so stupid?"

I don't remember what he said, but it was probably something to the effect that I was afraid to fight.

I was under the mistaken impression that the longer things went on without anyone attacking me, the more likely the whole thing would blow over, so I didn't let up.

"Bob," I said, keeping the focus on him and using his name as often as I reasonably could, "I don't see what you get out of this. Beating me up isn't worth getting suspended from the Scouts, or getting kicked out of school, or maybe even getting arrested."

I looked around at the group and realized that there was one other person in the group I recognized. He was in my grade level, but was small and thin for his age. Because he was the only one in this group who knew me, I assumed, probably correctly, that he instigated this.

"Bob," I said, "I know what Rickie wants out of this. I think he's got a crush on you, and he'd get excited watching you and some other guy fight." I had no basis for saying that, and fifty or so years later, I am embarrassed at appealing to the fear of homosexuality that frightened young males back then so much. But my father had pounded into me that you have to do the best you can with the tools you've got, and back then, that tool was *always* available.

Several guys in the group immediately began teasing Rickie, asking him if what I said was true. I took that as a good sign. I believed, or hoped, it meant they were looking for a way to defuse the situation.

"Is he really a Boy Scout?" I asked. "I bet he's a Webelo." A Webelo was the most advanced level for a Cub Scout, a transitional phase to the Boy Scouts. So, calling Rickie a Webelo played on his size and the fact that he looked younger than he was. But in context, it also unfairly suggested that he was insufficiently manly.

That deflected another round of teasing away from me toward one of their group. In retrospect, it also amounted to a form of bullying on my part that I don't feel good about, but at the time, my attitude was, *hey, he and his pals started this, I didn't.*

The confrontation didn't end on that note.

Bob took up my challenge and said that what he'd get out this was the opportunity to knock me on my ass. Or something to that effect.

I repeated that I had no desire to fight him and took a step back, trying to put myself out of reach of the quick shove that usually preceded a school yard fight.

"Come on," he said, "I'll fight you. Just you and me."

That was the problem with singling out one guy to fight. It implied you were going to fight him. That was, I suppose, better than having ten guys beat the crap out of you, but I had been hoping, maybe unrealistically, for an ending in which no one beat the crap out of me.

"Bob, I have no interest in fighting you," I countered. "Go fight someone who actually wants to get kicked out of school."

Schools back then did not have programs to deal with bullying. They had one rule: If you got in a fight, you got punished. If some bully beat you up and a teacher saw it, you both got punished. That was the rule.

Bob moved into a boxing stance and put up his fists.

"Bob," I repeated, "I have no interest in fighting you."

"You're afraid," he said, or something to that effect.

"Yeah, that's right. I'm afraid. I'm crying like a little girl."

"I'm going to knock you on your ass if you don't fight me."

"I don't want to fight you. I have no reason to fight you," I insisted. My father, however, had another street-smart rule about fights. He didn't care about school policy. His rule was: I needed to learn to stand up for myself. So, I added, "But if you attack me, I *will* defend myself."

I moved into a wrestling crouch, or at least a very tentative, wimpy version of one. That was a big mistake. I should have had the courage to maintain my "not interested" posture.

In any event, that left him in a boxing stance and me in wrestling stance.

"You afraid to fight with your fists?" he taunted.

"I don't want to hurt you," I said.

"Okay," he said, "we can wrestle." He moved into a wrestling posture.

"Or, we could act like we're not afraid of peer pressure," I said, "and decide not to be stupid." I stood up more-or-less straight, but kept my arms extended in case he attacked.

He stepped forward and attempted to shove me.

Using one of the simplest moves I'd read about in the judo book, I swung my left leg behind his right leg, bending his leg at the knee from behind. That left him standing on one leg, leaning forward. I pulled him toward me and then lowered him to the ground. He ended up face down on the sidewalk, with me kneeling on his back, twisting his arm behind his back.

"Bob," I said, "I'm not mad at you, I don't have a grudge against you, and I don't want to fight you. So, here's what's going to happen. I'm going to let you up. You and your friends are going to leave.

Tomorrow, you can tell everyone how you beat the crap out of me. People will think you're an asshole, and I'm a nerd, and we'll all be happy."

I let him up. I expected him to bluster and make some verbal threats, but I thought it was all over.

It wasn't. He couldn't, from his point of view, let things end with him being humiliated. He probably figured I'd been lucky and wouldn't be able to pull off whatever I'd done twice.

I *know* that's what *I* was thinking.

He came at me again, and I made the same move, and once again we ended up with him face down on the ground and me kneeling on his back, twisting his arm behind his back.

"Bob," I said, "I don't want to fight you. I don't want to hurt you. But I'm done. I am going to let you up, but it's over. *Don't* try that again. I gave his arm a little push toward his shoulder blades, just enough to demonstrate that I could inflict some serious pain if I wanted to, and then I let him up.

I was thinking, *Holy Shit, don't come at me again.* Even though I had practiced this move with my cousin in Florida, I knew I was lucky to pull it off the first time, and the second time was beyond lucky. *Next time, he's going to figure it out, and I'm going to be in a world of hurt.*

To my surprise, he asked me to show him how I took him down.

That seemed like a really, really bad idea. Because as soon as I did, he or one of his buddies would want to try it on me.

I said no and told him to go home.

He came at me again, and I made the same move, and he went down again. But this time, I followed through the way the judo book showed, with his arm twisted and my leg pressing against it, threatening to break his arm in way that would have been extremely painful.

"Bob," I said, "you're going to promise, if I let you up, to walk away. Or I'm going to break your arm. Which is it going to be?"

I think he muttered a curse or threat, but his buddies were talking louder, assuring me it was over, that he'd walk away this time.

I helped him up.

He and his buddies left.

You might think that would be every adolescent geek's fantasy come true, and in a way, I suppose it was. But the whole thing left its emotional scars on me. *Sure, it was great that I had handled myself okay, at least by the standards of the time, but why had they singled me out to begin with? What was it about me that brought this out in other people? Did they attack me because I was a socially awkward geek? Or because I was an insecure jerk?*

I'd like to say that I learned some important lesson from this incident, and that it gave me the self-confidence to fulfill my childhood dream of becoming a physicist. But that's not what happened. Instead, one day in algebra or calculus class, the teacher began talking about imaginary numbers and irrational numbers. *Imaginary* numbers? *Irrational* numbers? I realized in a moment that I did not have the math aptitude to be a physicist.

And in my high school physics class, I learned that electrons weren't just little particles whirling around the nucleus of the atom, as they had been in the science books I had read on my own. *No*, in grown up physics, electrons were *either* particles *or* waves, depending on the situation or how you thought about them. *Wait a minute. Huh?*

You couldn't even say that an electron was *here* or it was *there*, and how much it weighed, and which direction it was going, and how fast it was going. The best you could do was pick some, but not all, of those parameters and then give the odds, the probability, you were right. Odds are, it's *here*, but it's within the range of probabilities that it's *there somewhere.*

So, I was living in a world in which school yard fights were not imaginary and had rules, but numbers were *imaginary* and *irrational?* Electrons were both particles *and* waves, and were probably *here*, but statistically might be *there?* And they were either a particles or waves depending on how you chose to think about them?

I decided – not then, but in time – that if I wanted to live in a world in which there *were* rules, I should become a lawyer. The law is the law. Nothing's imaginary or irrational, except perhaps your opponent's argument. And justice isn't something that's different depending on how you choose to think about it. *Right?*

TRIPLE LOSSES: EXXON AND THE US

By *Alvena Stanfield*

LOSS 1:

Darren Woods, Exxon's new chief executive smiles from page B6 of the Wall Street Journal's March 2, 2017 Business News. The article states Exxon will invest a fourth of its [projected $22 billion net income] budget, $5.5 billion dollars, obtaining shale oil reserves. CEO Woods explains: "Obtaining shale oil and natural gas is a quicker process than previous methods" and Exxon "expects to obtain forty dollars per barrel from this venture." According to Woods the three states: Texas, New Mexico and North Dakota can produce six billion barrels of oil and natural gas.

"Obtaining shale oil and natural gas" sounds so innocuous, so beneficial, doesn't it? No mention of the words "induced earthquakes" or "fracking" appears. "Induced earthquake" is used by the U.S. Geological Survey (USGS) to evaluate recent increasing earthquake occurrences. Fracking is a dirty word in the oil-for-profit and in the environmental worlds. That's why it so seldom appears in articles where oil magnates are interviewed.

So, why is fracking unmentionable? Because: To reach oil-saturated shale, hydraulic pressure is forced into the solid lithosphere (tectonic plates) to break them, vacuum the pieces and crush them to squeeze out the oil. This equates to a disturbance of the lithosphere. When the lithosphere shifts, its tectonic plates' movement triggers earthquakes.

A quick update in geology here: Our thin layer of soil and oceans are above our lithosphere (solid rock). Below that is a layer similar to bubble gum. It is solid yet moldable. Below that is the more liquid oil and natural gas. Below that is the core, the extremely hot center caused by the earth's rotation and degrading Isotope 13.

Studying this the U.S. Geological Survey (USGS), a governmental agency reports its observations and calculations. It offers only statistics based on its observations, not opinion, not recommendations and not conclusions. One of its diverse responsibilities is to monitor earthquake activity. It has identified earthquake hazards in the United States and provides a color chart of those hazards: http://USGS.gov/earthquake hazards. USGS is also conducting an ongoing study of increased earthquake occurrences.

For centuries shifting tectonic plates and earthquakes have occurred naturally. Triggers for this shifting are volcanic eruptions, a tectonic plate sliding above or below a continent's edge, and under-ocean volcanic eruptions that spread the seafloor's lithosphere. Each occurs naturally. These plates also shift by one tectonic plate stepping forward while the one alongside it remains in place. Those are called transform shifts.

According to the USGS the number of earthquakes per year is increasing. Its ongoing study compares previous years to the present incidences of earthquakes. Its website, shown below states:

Between the years 1973–2008, there was an average of 21 earthquakes of magnitude three and larger [M3+] in central and eastern United States. This rate has ballooned to over 600 M3+ earthquakes in 2014 and over 1000 in 2015. Through August 2016, over 500 M3+ earthquakes have occurred.

Its detailed analyses are shown:

https://earthquake.usgs.gov/research/induced/

USGS reports make no accusations against the oil industry's fracking. Exxon and other companies participating in shale extraction methods deny accelerated incidences of earthquakes located near shale extraction sites.

Do the oil industry's denials echo the twentieth-century denials of the tobacco industry?

We all know how that worked out.

LOSS 2:

To understand fracking versus drilling methods, let's review the oil industry's past method. A relatively small drill hole through the earth's layers extracted oil by pumping it to the surface, leaving the lithosphere intact except at the drill site.

With the fracking process, by bursting the solid rock lithosphere, oil can be obtained faster, cheaper than the drilling method but inflicts more damage to the lithosphere. That includes the lithosphere below the states mentioned in the Wall Street Journal: Texas, New Mexico, and North Dakota. Take a moment to carefully review the USGS map illustrating "danger zones for earthquakes:" (https://i.kinja-img.com/gawker-media/image/upload/s--MY-f7Nr0/c_scale,fl_progressive,q_80,w_800/s2qeivsfeo6qsdsegmuq.jpg) The purple and red zones are the most earthquake-prone areas in the US. Not surprising, the Western coast where horrific earthquake damage has occurred in California and Alaska glow purple and red. Kentucky is included in a hazardous zone (New Madrid fault).

Now take a hard second look at the states mentioned by Exxon's Darren Wood in the Wall Street Journal article. They are shown in an earthquake-endangered zone. Exxon's plan for bursting the Texas, New Mexico and North Dakota's lithosphere, to provide profits greater than $22 billion net annually, is likely to cost the residents of those states far more than that in losses of life, limb and property.

Mr. Woods explained Exxon's attitude in the article: "Obtaining shale oil and natural gas is a quicker process than previous methods." The article explains that his is essential for Exxon due to its shrinking profits and rising debt experienced between 1999 and 2016. Exxon's net profit in 1999 was $82 billion and $7.8 billion in 2016, while Rex Tillerson was chief executive. This estimated leap from $7.8 billion to

$22 billion net profit apparently depends on fracking.

At an Exxon analyst meeting in New York, in his first official meeting, Chief Executive Darren Woods, stated, "Our job is to compete and succeed in any market, irrespective of conditions or price," According to Woods the three states [Texas, New Mexico and North Dakota] can produce six billion barrels of oil and natural gas. The unit price mentioned in the article is forty dollars per barrel (6 billion x $40 = $24 billion dollars).

Could Exxon's repaying debt and being able to "...succeed in any market, irrespective of conditions...." And Exxon's profiting more billions justify risking our earth's underground integrity and stability?

LOSS 3

The Wall Street Journal's March 12, 2017 article states Darren Woods replaced Rex Tillerson as Exxon's CEO when President Trump named him Secretary of State. Tillerson was Exxon's CEO over the seventeen-year period between 1999 and 2016. While he was at the helm of Exxon, in 1999 it had $82 billion net profit. Exxon had steady losses, dropping to $7.8 billion net profit by 2016: a 90% loss of net income. 90%. Considering the United States' fiscal deficits, can the US afford him?

ABOUT
THE
AUTHORS

KIMBERLY ARMSTRONG

Kimberly Armstrong hails from Chicago. She is a poet, and also pretty good at writing essays--though she rarely gets around to that. She concerns herself with society, inequality, humanism, and Judaism. She is a Reconstructionist. She loves reading and singing. She also enjoys learning languages, travel, and "natural house" design. She is in love with love.

JENNY BREEDEN

Jenny Breeden was born and raised in Erlanger, Kentucky, and moved to Covington in 1985. She has three grandchildren. She enjoys traveling, photography, scrapbooking, and crafts such as jewelry making, crocheting, cross-stitch, and painting. A Northern Kentucky University alum, Jenny is an avid reader and considers herself a lifelong learner. She's written poetry and short stories over the years, including mysteries, historical fiction and person narratives.

She joined the Covington Writers Group in 2014 and has been a driving force in getting their anthologies published each year. By sharing her knowledge and experience in the self-publishing world through workshops and seminars, she's helped others move forward with getting their dreams in print.

LESLIE BUSH

Leslie Bush has lived all her life in Covington, graduated from Holmes High School in '84 and NKU in '88 with a Bachelor's Degree in English. Her interest is in 19th Century British and French literature and Fantasy and Science Fiction.

She has been writing since she was 11, and she writes primarily in the Fantasy genre with a twisted sense of humor. She prides herself on her black humor. What can she say; she's a bloody goth. It is a world of magic and fiction. Anything is possible.

MIKEY CHLANDA

Mikey Chlanda is the author of more than a dozen books, ranging from firefighting to joke books to heist novels. He was born in and raised in New York City. Chlanda came to Yellow Springs to go to Antioch College. When Maples (the college fire department) found out he had been an ER Tech in a Manhattan emergency room, they made Chlanda join. Chlanda fell in love with the fire service and after college, he joined the village fire department, retiring as a lieutenant due to injuries.

Chlanda started writing his first book, "Maples: A History of the Antioch College Fire Department", a history of the only student-run fire department in the world, for something to do in between surgeries and rehab. When it sold over 2600 copies the first year, he thought he could make a living at this writing thing.

As well as writing books, Chlanda also writes regularly for Huffington Post, ESPN.com, Writers Weekly, and Forbes.com, along with other sites and magazines sporadically. He was a featured speaker at the 2017 Indie Author Day event at the Boone County Library. He's also given talks at the Kenton County Library, Louisville Library, and various fire museums.

PATTI KAY EMERSON

Patti Kay Emerson was born in September 1960 in Covington, Kentucky, where she lived until she moved to Florence, Kentucky in 2015. She graduated from Gateway Community and Technical College in 2010 with a 3.4 GPA with an Associate in Art Degree. She was also inducted into Phi Theta Kappa, an international honor society for two-year colleges.

BRAD HUDEPOHL

R. Brad Hudepohl grew up in the western part of Cincinnati He attended Western Hills High School. He has a Bachelor of Arts in German from The Ohio State University and a Bachelor of Science in Pharmacy from the University of Cincinnati. He had worked as a pharmacist since 1976 and is currently retired.

ELLE MOTT

Elle Mott writes creative nonfiction with an emphasis on memoir. Publications include a national news magazine, literary journals, and inclusion in local area anthologies. She writes about homelessness, recovery, college activism, and humanism.

She is a 2010 college graduate near Seattle, Washington. Her work as a page with The Public Library of Cincinnati and Hamilton County is her livelihood, while her writing is her passion. She values her friendships, her pet finches, and her community of neighbors in Northern Kentucky.

Elle hangs out on Facebook at ellemott.author and Twitter @NovElleMott and is in several online writing groups. Her website is www.ellemott-author.com/

L. N. PASSMORE

As soon as she could walk, L. N. Passmore toddled into the sea. At age six she got lost in the woods, perfect for communing with tree spirits and departed ancestors. No wonder living in the Appalachians made forested mountains—filled with secret music and light—her muses. Her beloved cats, dogs, and horse became wise counselors.

She has lived, worked, and traveled all over USA, from Alaska and the Navajo Nation in Arizona to the Atlantic Coast; and the UK, from John o' Groats to Land's End. Her first of many extended trips to the Scottish Highlands brought her home to a land new to her eyes but not her soul. Visits to the western isles: Mull, Iona, Staffa, and Skye, where the veil between worlds is the thinnest, revealed the truth of Old Powers.

Passmore's *Wayward Wulves Beware*, Book 1 of the Eye of the Wulf Series, is for sale, hardcopy and e-book, at <u>amazon.com</u> and soon to be available at Barnes and Noble and other local bookstores. Visit her website, Moving Mountains at: <u>www.lnpassmore.com</u> to read her *Tales of Appalachia, Tales of Lisnafaer,* and her Blog: *Mountain Musings.*

GARY REED

Gary Reed is the author of the legal thriller <u>A Fatal Cell Phone Video</u> and the medical/legal thriller <u>The Blockbuster Drug</u>.

Gary Reed draws on his extensive legal experience in his writing. He practiced law in a large law firm and later in an in-house capacity. Throughout his career, he managed litigation and investigations across the country.

He has always been interested in writing. He wrote for and edited his high school and college newspapers and wrote professional articles in his areas of legal specialty.

Gary relies on a robust network of beta readers to make sure his works are easy to read and enjoyable. He is also an active participant in two writing groups.

ALVENA STANFIELD

Alvena Stanfield is a published author of fiction and non-fiction stories. She has recently dabbled in teaching a multi-media experience in all genres and in screen writing. She attends Northern Kentucky University and is on the Scholars List. Most recently her interests are historic fiction set in the mid-nineteenth century western frontier. Her novel Frontier Messenger is expected to be available through Amazon in 2018.

To receive a pre-pub chapter, contact 859-409-3434 or stanfieldwrites@gmail.com.

CONTACT US

Connect with us at:

CovingtonWritersGroup@outlook.com

and

SeagullProductionsLLC.com

www.ingramcontent.com/pod-product-compliance
Lightning Source LLC
Chambersburg PA
CBHW020618250626
47154CB00004B/1573